HEAVENLY

RHYTHM & BLUES

POEMS 1982 - 1993

HARALD WYNDHAM

<u>HEAVENLY RHYTHM & BLUES, Poems 1982 - 1993</u>

by Harald Wyndham

Published by **Blue Scarab Press** in November, 1993

Copyright 1993 by Harald Wyndham

ISBN 0-937179-08-6

Cover photographs by Peter Vincent, copyright 1989
published with permission

Manufactured by **Litho Printing**, in Pocatello, Idaho

Certain poems were originally published in the following magazines or anthologies: *Boise Magazine; Eleven; Limberlost Review; Mountain Standard Time; Nexus; Plough: Northcoast Review; Puerto del Sol; The Rolling Coulter; Timberline; White Clouds Revue; <u>Eight Idaho Poets</u>, U. of Idaho Press; <u>Famous Potatoes: Southeast Idaho Poetry</u>, Blue Scarab Press; <u>Idaho's Poetry: a Centennial Anthology</u>, U. of Idaho Press; <u>The Literature of Idaho, an Anthology</u>, Boise State University Press; <u>When You Love Me There Is One Universe</u>, Blue Scarab Press.*

NOTICE: THE OCCASIONAL USE OF EXPLICIT LANGUAGE <u>MAY BE OFFENSIVE TO SOME READERS.</u> This book is <u>NOT RECOMMENDED</u> for children.

Years ago I was playing guitar with Jane's cousin Bill Jolliff and his new wife, Brenda, at a family reunion in a city park in LaRue, Ohio. Bill told me a story about going to a reunion of Brenda's family. They have so many relatives that they rent a church camp. Bill told me that when they gathered in the cafeteria for breakfast or lunch, someone would raise the first line of a song, and by the second line <u>everyone</u> in the room would be singing along--<u>in harmony.</u> It made the hair stand up on my neck. That, I said to myself, is what it must be like in Heaven.

"I'm just a guy with a crooked tie." That line from an old Tex Beneke song has also been running through my head for years until a poem finally pearled around it. Writing and self-publishing poetry in a place like Pocatello, Idaho, one not only understands, but comes to embrace the role of being "just a guy with a crooked tie," a face in the crowd, just like the next person. Life is less complicated when nobody worries about what you are doing. There remains, of course, a desire to be listened to by someone who knows your thoughts and shares your passion. Perhaps in Heaven.

Walter started from Paumanok. I started from Pocatello. When we moved out with the kids in 1971, we didn't plan to stay. But we settled down, raised the kids and grew to love this small city, split by the railyards, between two knobby mountain ranges. We have lived here now longer than anywhere else in our lives. I learned to be a writer in Pocatello, as well a husband, and a father (and grandfather). Now, seventeen books of poems later, Jane and I have celebrated our silver anniversary, the kids have grown up, graduated from Idaho State, married wonderful people and started careers and families. "Everything goes onward and outward-- nothing collapses."

<u>Heavenly Rhythm & Blues</u> is a backyard jam session of a book. Over the years I have been lucky to occasionally sit in with some very talented musicians where we play around the circle with each one leading a song in turn. We jump from railroad songs to murder ballads to the Carter family to Leadbelly blues and Hank Williams, Dylan, John Prine with absolute freedom, enjoying the diversity of choice and memory. It is unorganized, spontaneous and full of contradictory styles and themes. Yet every voice is listened to and honored, as they are, perhaps, in Heaven.

A decade ago I published my first decade of poems, <u>Cheap Mysteries</u>, a crowded, crammed gathering of miscellaneous pieces from the first ten years of writing. Now, twelve years later, <u>Heavenly Rhythm & Blues</u>, a second "decade." I don't know how many more decades I dare count on.

If I am blessed to see the odometer turn over into a new millennium, I hope it is a time of increasing peace and compassion among all peoples and nations, to balance out this century of global slaughter. I hope there is still an earth to pass on to my grandson's children, with trees, clean water, fresh air and species in abundance, such as we still take for granted in Idaho. I hope that our interests turn away from the material, the physical and violent, and that we choose instead to explore the spiritual dimensions of living, seeking simplicity on the outside and celebrating complexity within. Now that would be something worth living to see.

And If I get put on the bench before then, well, I just hope I can bring my Gibson Blue Ridge Custom along. I'll sit there in an outrageous hawaiian shirt, under a

glowing tree with the beautiful tiny leaves that hang down like the hair of a god-
dess, singing rhythm and blues and drinking a tall, cool glass of holy water . . .
Perhaps I'll even be able to figure out bar chords in Heaven. And when the rest of
you show up, we'll have a blast, digging each other's soul music for eternity.

And if there isn't a Heaven, that's alright, too. Say it's an underground metro-
karma-exchange station crowded with gray-faced commuters. We'll lean against
the wall, smoking unfiltered cigarettes, banging out steel string rhythms and wailing
our human blues. Count on it.

Don't forget your harmonica.

                                        -- Harald Wyndham

DEDICATION

This book is dedicated to singers and pickers,
fiddlers, sidemen, slidemen, hammer-dulcimers,
sweet gospel harmony, jammers, buckdancers &
all those who have let me sit in with them . . .

For Mike Bernard, first and foremost, leading the way

For Bill and Brenda, and the circle unbroken

For Baller, Orr, Finlayson and the good old days

For Ray, Jackie, Clifford, Charles every other Wednesday

For Steve Eaton, Tim Hodgson -- major leaguers

For Jeff, Randy and Sally, sagegrass and yodels

For Will Peterson, stompin at the Walrus

For joyful noises, Mary, Kerry and Sandy

And for my son, Jonathon, who carries it on

And son-in-law John and grandson Dylan, drummin . . .

STARTING FROM POCATELLO

Starting from Pocatello, with it's broken streets,
      it's migrant trees and sidewalks shoved up by frost,
      with the alleys unpaved, dusty and full of holes,
      where I have walked with the dog and without the dog
      in late afternoon and at night under the moon
      with hungry poems tugging hard at the leash . . .

Starting from Pocatello, with its worn-down peaks,
      cupping their snowbanks against the April sun,
      and Scout's skewed hump white-blue on the horizon,
      the modest rock-strewn path along Red Hill
      above the cemetery, where the wind blows hard
      and the town spreads out serene across the valley,
      sliced by the gash of the railyard, smoky and brown.

Starting from Pocatello, in my twenty-fifth year,
      with young wife and toddlers and a blue microbus,
      coming to teach for a few years, then to return,
      and instead staying here forever, as so many do,
      seduced by blue skies, openness, anything goes--
      the chance to be my own person and start life anew.

Starting from Pocatello, where progress is glacial
      in this blue-collar town with a laid-back attitude,
      hometown to bishops, birchers, hippies and beats,
      vote-the-man-not-the-party individualist dreamers,
      and writers and artists, musicians by the score,
      with our unmowed yards and gardens of marigolds,
      unbothered, unnoticed, happily left to ourselves
      in small basement rooms in this unimproved town,
      where we gossip together at the grocery store
      about the crowded, arrogant cities we escaped.

Starting from Pocatello, with my blue notebook
      determined to write a poem a day for five years,
      like walking cross country beyond all boundary lines
      until I came to an unsettled place in my mind,
      with mountains and rivers as wild as Idaho,
      and the sheer drop-off where cliff swallows soar,
      where the elk shakes his rack at the farmland below,
      and I stood like the only soul in a thousand miles,
      where for the first time I knew that I belonged.

Starting from Pocatello, in my basement room,
      in the night, by lamplight, with everyone asleep,
      with notebooks and keyboard and jazz on the radio,
      cool air slipping its cut grass smell in the window,
      and the boxcars singing retarded whalesongs,
      I hammered my agon and ecstasy onto the page,
      in freedom and happiness, lucky to be in this place
      in this country in this unbroken period of peace,
      in Idaho, in a state of undeserved grace.

Starting from Pocatello, who could ask for more,
          assuming you don't want much in the way of culture,
          but are happy with snowfall and temperatures below
          absolute zero when an Alberta Clipper comes down
          and the snow is so freeze-dried it squeaks
          and they don't plow the side-streets for weeks
          because plowing costs money and everyone
          would rather owe money on 4-wheel drive pickups
          than pay another cent in city tax--besides
          anyplace worth going is worth going on skis,
          but sitting at home by the woodstove is the best.

Starting from Pocatello, where everyone is radical,
          writing vociferous letters to the newspaper
          that others take issue with vociferously
          or at city council meeting free-for-alls,
          declaring Pocatello a "nuclear free zone"
          or banning chemicals that destroy the ozone
          or displaying the Ten Commandments in public
          or walking around looking "peeved and dejected"
          which is a misdemeanor here, so smile, damn you.

Starting from Pocatello, with its cowboy bars
          and its cowboy bards reciting their rhymed couplets
          and couples in cowboy hats dancing the western swing
          or the twostep to Country Gold at the Green T,
          and the college boys banging guitar at the First,
          and the homegrown tenor in concert singing Aida,
          and mainstreet crowded with dancers one summer night
          and the poets drinking beer in the Roundup Room
          after a wild time reading the roof off the Walrus.

Starting from Pocatello, after working all day,
          I walk the midnight streets like I own the town,
          reciting my favorite poems at the top of my head
          until I come to the house where my children sleep
          and I sneak in quietly not to awaken the dog
          and slip under covers beside the woman I love,
          sharing with her every nightmare, every heartbeat,
          every naked and honest syllable spoken in dreams,
          in this most real place in the universe to live,
          I give myself to whatever comes with each breath,
          hoping with all my heart "to cease not till death."

A BRIEF CAREER IN VACUUMS

there i was carrying this
hoover vacuum cleaner in one hand
and a briefcase crammed with
order forms in the other
down some sad, broken street
in a city of smog and sagging wires
past the neon bars where
the husbands of my victims
played pool all afternoon
while i wooed their unhappy women
with my big sucking machine,
except after knocking my
knuckles raw on two
hundred grimy apartment doors
lugging that mother up five flights
until one of them opened up
and there was this big
black lady with arms thick as hams
and her hair in curlers
looking at me like i had leprosy
and asking "whatchuwant?"
so that instead of
pouring my little bag of dirt
on the shag carpet where three kids
crawled around in diapers
to demonstrate the wondrous suck
of the hoover upright i just
gave her the damned thing
and floated away out
the window letting
america suck me
like a hair
ball into
the enormous
vacuum of her soul.

AMERICAN DREAMSONG

one day in april
i came home for lunch
and started putting new strings
on my guitar, like it had been
years since i picked it up
what with work, the kids
and everything, and
maybe it was the sun shining
on the new leaves of the lilac
or sparrows jabbering away
in the spruce tree
that made me feel like
making music all day
so once i got those medium gauges
screwed down and tuned up
i couldn't stop playing,
you know what I mean?
when my wife came home from work
there i was, singing the blues
and still not tired of it
though my fingers ached
and she could tell
it didn't much matter to me
if i lost the job, the insurance, all of it,
just so i could play one more
dave van ronk tune
and holler my head off
uninhibited and free,
like a sparrow in a spruce tree.

"OVER 90 BILLION SERVED"

You know what I'm talking about.
       90 billion hamburgers in forty years.
       I was in high school when they hit one million.
       My kids were born at 50 and 100 million.
       We moved to Idaho around one billion, give or take.
       We've lived here now for 89 billion hamburgers.

Over 90 billion served. How to measure it?
       At two ounces per hamburger, it's 12 billion pounds.
       At 500 pounds per steer, it's 24 million steers.
       or 600,000 steers per year (and that's no bull).

Over 90 billion served. Laid end to end
       in some classic metaphor of statistics,
       they would blanket the earth from pole to pole
       twice, like a two-ply crocheted sweater,
       or stretch to the moon and back 24 times.

Over 90 billion served. Served to whom?
       In the past 40 years, world population has grown
       from 3 billion to 5 billion people, give or take.
       That's 22.5 hamburgers per person, on average.
       Has everyone had their fair share? Have you?
       At 150 pounds, you weigh 1,200 hamburgers.
       Some have eaten their weight in hamburgers--twice.
       Still, whole populations are waiting to be served,
       and we are catching up with them at great speed
       in a perfect metaphor of democratic capitalism
       arching golden from sea to shining sea.

Over 90 billion served. And that's not counting
       the other guys, the competition. Add them in
       and we've got perhaps 150 billion served--
       as many as the stars in the Milky Way--
       and that's not counting the shakes and fries.

Over 90 billion served. Where are they now?
       Who knows what happened to all of them? Do you?
       I figure 45 billion flushes, give or take a few.
       And is the world a better place? Do we have peace?
       Is mankind healthier, happier or better fed?
       Can you sleep without fear in your own bed
       knowing in every minute in every hour
       4,281 hamburgers are being devoured? Can you?
       Of course you can. After all, you're only human.

Over 90 billion served. Perhaps at 100 billion,
       (before the end of this decade) the Lord will come
       with hosts of angels ushering in the Millennium,
       and each of them will order just one . . . "to go."

THE DECIMAL SYSTEM

dear gentle
openminded reader who
in this book will encounter
perhaps one-tenth of all the poems
i have published over the past two decades
which represent less than one-tenth
of the poems in the notebooks,
theselves scarcely a tenth of the
urges ideas musings hungers fantasies
loves griefs angers jokes polemics
lusty dreams and desperations that rise
like the proverbial one-tenth tip
of a titanic, gleaming iceberg over
the fathomless depths of a single
human soul,
           what hope have you
in your brief skim across the surface
of libraries, a few anthologies, one or two
collections from rare book rooms and perhaps a few
yellowed reviews of out-of-print chapbooks,
not to mention notebooks, family letters,
interviews with surviving children
and serious scholarly studies
for the purpose of career
or finishing a degree
or just wierd curiosity
to understand at
best more than
one-tenth of
one percent
of who
I am?

good luck.

ONE MORE DAY IN PARADISE

if i can just
hold it together for
one more day get a few things
done get my desk cleaned chores done
so it feels like a circle in my
head if i can just hold it
together until i'm dead
so it doesn't ravel
apart too soon
so the pain doesn't come
washing everything back into the sea
like sandcastles these small poems
these ambitious songs if i can
hold my marriage my life
together one more day
with string with
masking tape
bandages
with hands
that tremble sometimes
holding each other if we can
just keep holding each
other we can survive
without drowning
or divorce disease
unspeakable catastrophe
these last few twenty years or so
with dignity and independence
in our own homes like we
always dreamed our
lives should have been before
we were born without this
constant pain these
arguments this
stress of
living together if
we can just hold hands
through one more peaceful day
as survivors comrades even
friends finally if this
can be done o let us
do it together
now today
please

SHOES

After father died,
we cleaned out the closet
where all his shoes waited neatly in pairs
like dancing couples sitting awkwardly on chairs
or taxies at a train station without fares,
useless without somebody needing them.

Father never wore out shoes.
He was a frugal man, raised in the Depression.
Even when they were too scuffed for church
and too worn out to be resoled,
he wore them to paint in.

I don't think it really hit home--
that he was dead and buried in the ground--
until I saw those brown wingtips and realized
his fingertips would never tie them on again.

We took them to the Salvation Army Thrift Store
where they were unceremoniously tossed
onto shelves stacked to overflowing
with other people's displaced shoes,
reminding me of Buchenwald or Dachau.

They are so grotesquely silent,
like masks of some tragicomic chorus,
fixed eyes, mouths agape, and the limp tongue
lolling to one side of a fool's face,
feigning a shocked wisdom.

Yet it does make sense, somehow, this pile of shoes
abandoned by all those who leave the world,
as at the doorstep of a sacred house,
where one must enter barefoot
so as not to offend the
Creator of souls.

THE CHILDREN WHO CANNOT WRITE THEIR NAMES

look up at me with eyes full of expectation
as I leap around the classroom reading poetry.
They love it, instinctively digging the rhythms,
the circus music of this verbal high-wire act,
and would write poems of their own all day
out of the seamless sorrow of their lives,
poems of cigarette smoke and torn furniture,
loud arguments, endless television, alcohol, drugs,
poems pushed like shopping carts through supermarkets
at eleven thirty at night with mom and baby sister,
poems snoring on the couch with dad all afternoon
or red as menstrual roses, blue as violent violets,
white as sexual syrup coating the car commercials
and the funkiest rhythm and blues song ever sung,
except they cannot write down even their names,
cannot spell simple words or read sentences,
the brilliant minds with street-wise eyes,
these fifth-grade geniuses staring up at me
like some magic Houdini escape artist of poetry
skilled in the dance of secret syllables
who knows perhaps a clever exit door--
a metaphor--a ticket out of hell.

I mask my anger and my urge to cry.

I leave them laughing as I wave goodbye.

THE MIDDLE-AGED WHITE CHRISTIAN CONFRONTS THE MAN BEATING HIS WIFE IN THE SUPERMARKET PARKING LOT ONE SUMMER NIGHT

caught in my headlights
as i backed around
he drew back and punched her
with a roundhouse fist
then grabbed her by the hair
and slammed her face
against the pavement three
four times while i
in disbelief and not
able to move honked my
horn at him but could not
get out for fear of
that anger perhaps a
knife knowing for the love
of Christ i should be
beaten in her place
smashed killed
sat still
honking the damned
horn until three stock
boys pulled him off
before he beat her dead.

Lord,
    i am unworthy
who just went to
the grocery for
donuts, milk
& bread.

PICASSO DREAMS

i

they all looked
at the painting

some laughed
some cursed
some turned away

each understanding
in his own way

ii

a piano sonata
played in a green room

a blue rose opens
in your brain

iii

the third dream
was a dance
performed
for the person
i couldn't see
who somehow
controlled me

iv

broken face
facing front
and back you
are my face
broken by
time take eat

v

picasso paints
in the next room

goatfooted, horned
he dances wildly

FORTY-SEVEN ALTERNATIVES TO SEX

Mowing the lawn with a push mower.
Changing the oil in the pickup truck.
Hiking twenty miles into the mountains.
Baking bread and kneading the warm, moist dough.
Reading <u>War and Peace,</u> or <u>Dr. Zhivago.</u>
Taking the children to the zoo all day.
Eating five cones of fat free frozen yogurt.
Riding your skateboard through four-way stops.
Playing electric guitar full blast after midnight.
Playing acoustic guitar softly by yourself.

Playing flamenco guitar on your neighbor's lawn.
Breaking your neighbor's guitar against a tree.
Running twenty miles before breakfast.
Walking slowly with the dogs after supper.
Kicking leaves into the air as you walk the dogs.
Watching the full moon rise behind bare branches.
Watching the sunrise on a mountain top on your knees.
Planting petunias, allissum, geraniums and marigolds.
Picking ripe tomatoes and eating them on the spot.
Tuning the piano for the first time in fifteen years.

Reading the New York Times Review of Books.
Reading underground poetry magazines in a coffee shop.
Writing letters to the editor protesting everything.
Breaking off handfuls of warm bread and gnawing them.
Looking through leaves of the birch tree into the sky.
Searching the cemetery for unusual and poetic names.
Cleaning the chimneys before winter sets in.
Canning tomatoes, pickles, beets, corn and green beans.
Sitting for two hours in a warm, soaky bath.
Playing chess with your best friend in the city park.

Skipping flat stones on the mirrored face of the lake.
Shooting the middle-fork rapids in a white-water raft.
Ringing churchbells at noon or midnight for no reason.
Riding no hands without a helmet at breakneck speed.
Skiing through powder so deep you get lost in it.
Lying on a lawnchair listening to classical music.
Putting the final perfect stitches into a quilt.
Screaming your head off at the top of the ferris wheel.
Watching the sparks fly into the star-studded sky.
Playing bluegrass banjo and moaning the blues.

Gleaning potatoes, scrubbing, baking, eating them.
Catching a native cutthroat on a hand-tied hopper.
Going to bed early and sleeping in late.
Walking barefoot on wet grass on a blue summer morning.
Reading to children and grandchildren before bedtime.
Praising God for disasters that didn't happen.
Thinking up other alternatives for the rest of your life.

THE LONG RIDE INTO DEATH

I bought my ticket and said goodbye,
found my way to the first class compartment,
waved briefly to those weeping on the platform,
and then the train mercifully pulled out.

Alone and exhausted, with no more
decisions to make, trusting the machine
to take me to my final destination,
I let go of pain and relaxed,
sinking into a primal sleep
as the compartment rocked
from side to side
and my life passed by the window
with its blurred images of quaint towns,
telephone wires, smokestacks and tall trees
which I no longer cared to look at,
letting go of everything except
the lulling of the rails
and the rocking coach
carrying me beyond dreams
into the great mothering sleep song
the tunnel of all endings
and beginnings.

TO MAKE SPAGHETTI SAUCE

Begin with a glass of bardolino
red and dry as the thin blood of the Borgias;
begin with soil composted and mulched for decades
with fifty years of gardening to draw on;
begin with tomatoes and peppers saucy, acidic,
and fat-bellied onions bringing tears to the eyes,
and a few skinny zucchini like adolescent boys
and a handful of basil, rosemary, oregano
pulled from the border above the marigolds.

Begin with a clear blue Sicilian morning sky
with west wind washed clean of civilization
and sunflowers lifting their faces to the sun
and sparrows swooping between the apple trees
in a town like Pocatello, where Italians came
to work on the railroad over a century ago--
their gravestones with the porcelain photographs
gathered in small neighborhoods in the cemetery--
so that a spaghetti sauce is never out of place
but feels at home with Pavaroti on public radio.

Saute the onions in extra virgin olive oil
(because straight virgin is not pure enough),
add tomato sauce and paste, peppers, zucchini
and slices of big mushrooms, handfuls of spice,
a dash of cinnamon and a pinch of clove,
the four seasons of Vivaldi and a few motets
by Monteverdi sung expressively with vibrato,
and simmered for two hours until the house
is vibrating with fantastic, warm aroma.
Then add browned sausage, drained of all fat,
and leave to bubble on warm while the pasta cooks.

This, plus a table of family and friends,
long loaves of sourdough bread and a green salad,
with ice cream and coffee, just to make it nice
brings to a close another day in paradise.

"I'M JUST A GUY WITH A CROOKED TIE"

"I'm not much on looks,
"I'm just a guy with a crooked tie . . ."

-- Tex Beneke, Glenn Miller Orchestra

I'm just a guy with a crooked tie . . .
    standing in the crowd, watching the parade,
    holding one of my kids by the hand,
    the other perched on my shoulder, mussing my hair,
    an ordinary joe, with a wife and family,
    a small house in a normal neighborhood,
    a couple of dogs, a couple of dented cars,
    a lawn full of clover, crabgrass and dandelion,
    putting my hand on my heart as the flag goes by.

I'm just a guy with a crooked tie . . .
    the kind you meet in the supermarket after work,
    a bit fatigued and frazzled from the ten hour day,
    picking up pizza and softdrinks, bananas and bread,
    whatever my wife's list tells me to pick-up, I buy,
    plus anything exotic that happens to catch my eye,
    like kiwi, scandinavian crackers and Irish beer,
    because why should I work so hard and not be free?

I'm just a guy with a crooked tie . . .
    always in the background, off to one side,
    in the newspaper photograph or the crowd on t.v.
    where the rich and important somebodies process by,
    just like Kilroy and the great historical bum,
    I built the rock of ages and raised the rising sun,
    another nameless extra in the cast of thousands
    who fought the wars, laid the bricks of skyscrapers,
    added up the numbers and published the reports,
    fixed the plumbing, plowed fields and laid track,
    disappeared down that road without looking back.

I'm just a guy with a crooked tie . . .
    minor-league short-stop with a modest r.b.i.
    night-club comedian stuck on the borscht circuit,
    country band-leader, warming up main events,
    self-published poet and occasional novelist,
    summer-stock actor directing dinner theatre,
    high-school hero little league football coach,
    silver-tongued toastmaster at Kiwanis dinners,
    assistant under-secretary of an Overlord,
    official spokesperson of the great Unspeakable.

I'm just a guy with a crooked tie . . .
  at peace with myself and my place in life,
  content to be just another face in the crowd,
  while heroic persons pose for their photographs
  and video cameras suck the life from their souls
  sift it for scandal and scrutinize every hair
  in hopes that some awful human tragedy will appear
  to feed the insatiable "minds that want to know"
  while I who contain as much of eternity
  as anyone on earth, quietly pass by
  like a zen master--a guy in a crooked tie--
  seeking nothing and finding it everywhere.

I'm just a guy in a crooked tie . . .
  a hand on the wheel, a link in the chain,
  my face as inscrutable as a blank stone,
  seen in the mirror, impossible to explain,
  dancing through all my hundred-thousand forms,
  wearing the ritual masks of a shaman priest,
  feeding the multitudes with a few sardines,
  teaching disciples without speaking a word,
  disappearing one day without warning as I came,
  but leaving a telltale trace in the cloud chamber,
  to prove my existence and puzzle the scientists,
  while off in another corner, I am reborn.

I'm just a guy with a crooked tie . . .
  common as everyone, normal as nobody,
  helpful, friendly, easy to get along with,
  unknown as the grass and inscrutable as dust,
  sparkling with secrets just under the surface,
  all the wealth of the universe in my eyes,
  available to anyone passing by . . .

ELEGY AT THIRTY THOUSAND FEET

For C. P. Wyndham -- for fathers lost and found

Thirty thousand feet above Nebraska

    where my friend, Greg Kuzma, lives with his long grief

        for brother and father, I am flying home

      from the funeral of my brother-in-law, dead at fifty-seven

        under circumstances most difficult

          to comfort or explain,

            especially to his sons,

          young men now, the age of my own son,

        who sobbed at the casket and would not move away,

    thus honoring and grieving their lost father.

Nor could he have explained to them, nor anyone,

    the sadness, heavy as an anvil on the heart,

      that pulled him out of life,

        (a heaviness I know as well,

          having lost mother and father

        along with youthful vigor and health,

      my children growing into their lives

    as they ought to do, as I wish them to, as we did

twenty five years ago, escaping away to the west,

    with little thought for what our parents felt,

      though I feel it now, grieving for them also).

        Below, the River Platte, a silver thread,

      connecting these many flights across the country

to weddings, funerals and family reunions

over a quarter-century,

passing through the airport like a pilgrim,

one in a myriad of faces intent on destinations,

where sometimes in the swirling crowd I think I see

my father or brother or a friend from college

in the stranger ahead of me

(as if one could confront, like Odysseus,

one's own lost comrades at a terminal gate

by a streaked window, searching the eyes

for that spark of recognition)

but am always mistaken,

and relieved it is not true,

confrontation avoided and secure silence

folding me into a blend of anonymous bodies

so that I have no identity, no father, no family,

am a being without papers, travelling incognito

through a random selection of seating,

into the whine of great engines

that lifts me out of daily events

into this sunshot arena.

*

It was a "fiercely mourning house," as Dylan named it,

the family huddled together in loose tears,

and when I saw his face in the casket

I lost all composure and sobbed with them

riding the rich flood of memories,

stabbed by the mystery

of how life suddenly ends,

and the familiar face on the cushion

scarcely the person we knew

yet terribly all that is left

and no way to make peace with it

other than tears.

How we held onto each other,

working the long hours of the funeral,

receiving the hundreds of friends

in that surreal half-party around the body

smothered by baskets of flowers,

until feet, legs, back, hands and brain

were bone-weary numb,

worked to exhaustion,

honoring this person, this face,

holding back thought,

holding back anger and questions

and why did it have to happen

and how can you leave me like this?

You--husband/father/man/god/lifegiver--

stand up and answer!

where have you gone to?

how could you leave us?

didn't you love us?

how can we stand it

to close the lid on this casket

and lower you into this hole in the ground

and leave you alone every night?

*

The stewardess brings coffee.

I stare out the window

at the serene, creme-colored cloudbank,

cotton-fluff stretching toward all horizons,

like a Sunday school image of heaven,

where angels play harps for eternity.

Jesus, I say, wherever we go in our dying,

it cannot be this crystalline emptiness,

sunlit, serene, completely inhuman,

so cold it puts frost on the window.

Then C.P. is sitting beside me

(he has been dead six years now)

not as an old man with nosehairs

and earwax, coughing out warstories,

but rather the tall god from childhood,

thick-haired, lean-joweled, alive

smoking his unfiltered cigarettes

and surveying my poem (which he scarce

understands) with those gray-green eyes

as if wanting to comment on how well

I had mowed the lawn,

or perhaps, in this case,

wishing to bring me some message

that I was too young to understand

when he was moved to say it many years ago,

but can receive now, in this surreal place,

thirty-thousand feet above the battlefield.

Father, let's talk.

I know you lost your father

when he died two years after your birth,

or (as the gossip goes) abandoned the home,

leaving your mother to raise you alone,

though you never spoke of this

(as I was abandoned by my father, Gunter,

when you married mother and adopted me

though I never speak of it)

and can we now utter our sorrow?

Or would you prefer to judge me, as usual,

keeping that distance between us.

What proof of success can I offer?

Shall I show you your first grandson

grown-up, married and working?

Or your great-grandson with his proud penis?

What do you want from me, father, why are you here,

breathing your smoky breath into my face

as if around the kitchen table in the last years,

                        smoking cigarettes together,

                           drinking tea until midnight,

                              missing mother,

                        but not able to say so directly,

                  not able to spill out our grief,

            but keeping it between us like a saucer of ashes.

Peace, old man.   I have long since stopped fearing you,

            long since unplugged your power to punish me

                  with hands or with words,

                        yet I sit up with you now,

                           waiting for the history,

                        which is all you can give to me,

                  and making what peace can be made

between fathers and sons.

                              *

And Gunter, lost father I never knew,
            where can you fit into this elegy,
                  what place have you,
            who mother divorced after I was born
after warfare and sickness worked on you
            in a world I can never imagine--
                        did you forget about me?
            Or did you at night on your knees
pray to the great god of living and dead
            for my life and well being?
                  Did mother write you
                        when I walked and I talked
                  what my grades were in school
            or did you know nothing, ask nothing,
and how can I touch you, whose flesh I am,
            from this tall altitude of time,
                  in this rare atmosphere
                        of imagination?
                              In your cousin's house

                              at Garmisch-Partenkirchen
                  I saw your picture and the family tree
        where I have no place, although I am your heir,
              and the branches are all bare
                    after four hundred fifty years.
              I recognized my great grandmother's face
swarthy, darkly beautiful in an oil portrait,
              and felt a strange homecoming,
                    after forty years,
                          the prodigal returned
                  to a house full of relics
        and not even an elder brother left
  to curse my name. Father Gunter--
        here is my report: I am alright.
              The other man raised me,
                          the damned American soldier.
              I am his bastard now.
        That is what supposedly you said
  when washing your hands of my memory
        and never sought contact
                    unless mother hid it from me
                          revealing your existance
                    only on my twenty-first birthday
  in a letter filled with documents
and you already dead of appendicitus
        and we never spoke about you
                    it seemed too delicate
                          nor did I ask that man
              who raised me in your place
        what he thought of you--no,
I stuck it all deep in my travelling bag,
        bringing it out only now
              at thirty-thousand feet,
                    to hold in my fingers
                          and fold and unfold
                    and crush into a ball
              to throw out the window
  as if it were that easy
to get rid of you.

                              *

  And for my own son,
        Jonathon Russell, named
                    for neither father
        but for friends,
  (to give him a fresh start in this world)
        what kind of father
              have I been to you?
  When you were born
              it felt like the sun
                    exploded inside me

29

so happy and proud
that I weep even today
when I see you perform,
making music like I can only
dream, what scars
do you bear from my fathering?
We can't speak of it of course.
We share cigarettes outside,
in the backyard.
Although I have quit,
I smoke a butt with you
as with your grandfather
in a shared ritual mystery of manhood,
sacred smoke of the kiva fire
rising between us,
who are always inarticulate
about the important things
as with my brother-in-law those weekends
we stood out in the backyard
while our wives fixed dinner
talking football
instead of mentioning
our pain,
which our sons share
though they know only part of it
and will learn the rest later
a legacy passed on
from Adam's first failure
in loyalty and the loss of the garden.
It is failure
that binds us together
the pain we can't mention
standing outside together
in rain or snow, in isolate wilderness,
away from the women, around
the midnight table,
the scout campfire,
smoking forbidden cigarettes
and talking about nothing
under lost stars.
My son, this is your song, too.

*

kyrie elesion,
beautiful grandson,
gift of the universe,
rose of salvation
redeeming all failure,
only to look at you
gives me a blessing
and hope for mankind

despite every evil
the newspapers bring me,
i look in your eyes
and enter tomorrow
when i will be memory
and you will be father
carrying me forward
as i carry grandfather
into your future,
small seed and core,
center of destiny,
rose of salvation,
all of us lift you
high on our shoulders
dancing in sunlight
round in a circle
drumming our story
into your heartbeat
fathers and grandfathers
for five generations
forming your fingerbones
we are your heritage
rose of salvation
beautiful grandson
kyrie elesion

*

We start our descent
over west Colorado, banking gradually
to leave the ethereal,
re-enter reality,
our difficult lives
with no easy answers.
I sit by the window,
holding my head in my hands,
praying because praying
is all we can do for each other
in isolation, apart,
unable to touch,
unable to solve anything,
praying for miracles,
healing, forgiveness,
hoping we have not hurt anyone
more than forgiveness can heal.
Son, hear my prayer,
whispered in solitude
at this high altitude,
may you forgive me
all of the injuries
done out of ignorance

31

                    or misguided arrogance,
                              as I forgive
                    both of my fathers
                              as they forgive me.
                    I won't abandon you,
               as long as I live and breathe
          I will be there for you,
                    loving you, helping you
                                   survive the whirlwind
                              that tears apart each of us,
                    testing us, breaking us,
     making us doubt ourselves,
                    I will be there for you
                         in that fierce moment,
                              eye of the hurricane,
                    someone to talk to,
               hand to hold onto,
     if you will let me.

                              *

Father Gunter, I reach out to you
                         after your death
                    wanting to tell you
                         peace,
                                   peace, disturbed spirit,
                    no one lays blame on you,
               who fathered a son at the end of a war,
     going on where life guided you,
               Peace,
                         unknown lifegiver,
                              there was one moment
                                   when you were there for me,
                              so how can I hate you?
                    All else I needed
          I got from another.
     He is true father,
               steadfast, longsuffering,
                    whose last name I carry,
                         along with his teaching
                    while from you I have only chemistry.
     Peace.
               Be at peace, Gunter,
                         Rest in peace, father,
          whoever,
               wherever you are.

                              *

You come to me gently, C.P.

now that our battles are over,

like a great sky being in the darkness

surrounding the plane. I think of you

fondly, amazed at your

great self-restraint,

never in anger

naming me "bastard"

(though I gave you cause)

out of love for my mother

as well as for me

you treated me fairly

as one of your sons.

And you were there for me,

hairy shoulders, lean belly, deep voice,

booming out laughter at your own jokes,

and blue-streak curses during home repairs--

you taught me to laugh and curse,

you taught me to love verse,

reading "The Wreck of the Hesperus"

and "Hiawatha" in late evening lamplight,

and although you never threw a baseball

or came to the ballgames or watched me

win the 220 yard dash my senior year,

you performed well that night I told you

I had fathered a child, giving

      instead of the anger and lecture I dreaded,

         a quiet acceptance, as between men

            who have both fathered children,

         so that I was not ashamed to enter

      the common arena of toil and marriage

but went as with your blessing.

            Oh father,

      I remember the blessing I felt

         coming home for your last birthday,

            how we surprised you--

      all of your children,

      there on your doorstep--

giving back honor and love you scarce hoped

      to receive. It made it less painful

         to stand by your casket one month later

            receiving the entire community

         your life had touched.

      And one final blessing you gave me,

awaking at four in the morning after the funeral

      out of a dream where I held onto your leg

         as you came down the stairs

      and you bent down to help me let go

and your face was a young man's face.

      I trembled and wept long tears,

         touched by your presence,

and gently let go of you,

    who had already entered

the beautiful place.

*

We fasten our seat belts for final descent

    over the Wasatch range. The flight attendants

    make their frantic rounds.

In five minutes we'll be on the ground.

    I think of my brother-in-law's funeral,

        the generous words spoken for this man

        by those who knew him best

        and not at all,

        the great loneliness

    behind the mask of husband, father, friend,

how difficult it is--impossible--

    to share our thoughts with anyone,

        how even surrounded by those we love,

we do our crying alone,

    strong in our anger,

        weak in our pain.

    I think of C.P. in the night,

    sitting alone in a halo of lamplight,

    fastening colored stamps into his collection,

the way I sit at night in the basement room

filling page after page in a blue notebook,

and of the desperate look

I sometimes catch in the corner of my eye

while shaving at the mirror before work.

And all we have left is some hardware:

C.P.'s pocketknife I keep on my desk always,

and his woodworking tools with the striped handles

and my brother-in-law's masonic ring,

things that lived in dresser drawers for years

useless, except for the stored life

released by touching them,

talisman, carved bones,

shaman stones.

*

Coming down from heaven, the pressure builds

squeezing the busy world back into the brain,

until the skull seems ready to explode.

The heavy plane floats down on its cushion of air,

to touch the runway with a tiny bump

and then the tires and the turbines scream.

What can it mean,

to walk down the jetway and re-enter the stream

of fathers and sons and brother on all sides,

passing each other oblivious to what we share,

standing side by side in restrooms,

hurrying through crowded halls to catch a plane,

each one carrying a heavy bag of pain.

Yet given a few hours,

here at the airport between flights,

or, better, around a campfire in the night,

there is a time to listen and to speak,

time to tell war stories and bad jokes,

and funny memories of unforgotten days,

like my brothers and I tell stories of C.P.

and my son and his friends tell stories about me,

and through that process even the dead are present,

sitting against the wall of the smoky lodge,

as young voices recount ancient deeds

and fire-struck faces transform into masks

of nameless warrior ancestors and kings,

and no one is himself alone

but contains all generations

fathers and sons

present for that moment

when the dream comes alive in the fire

and sparks shower upward toward the Milky Way

and the skin drum is pounded and the dancers come

shambling and feathered, shaking their ankle bells

into the great circle, dancing the story we know

of the wounded eagle who falls down from the sky,

and each of us chanting sounds we have never forgotten

as we watch the god in us collapse and die

and be reborn again in a younger voice

to circle up and take his place in the sky

and this goes on forever, around and around,

the faces in shadows coming forth to the fire

so that we recognize each other

father, son and brother,

and put arms around each other,

singing and chanting

and moving our feet together

until the night wind blows the embers out

and we scatter into the dark again like torn leaves,

scarce recognizing each other at the crowded baggage claim

or later, in traffic, in steel vehicles at high speed, competing

for space to breathe and live and raise our sons,

we elbow our way forward into the world,

carrying our heavy bags,

as our fathers did,

coming back from places in the sky,

looking over our shoulders

to say goodbye.

STOMPIN' AT THE WALRUS

They come from far away and here they are.

They come from depths, rising at night
                like galaxies, like stars.

Suddenly they fill the sky like the Northern Lights
                and we walk out beneath them
                looking up amazed.

They streak a burning arc across the sky.

These poems, these hot rocks from heaven.

These poets, these starry messengers.

And we put them in our pockets to take home
                to display on the mantle like meteorites
                and tell stories--
                                wildly elaborated stories--
                about the night
                at the Walrus when
                poems fell into our lives

                changing everying.

CITY LIGHTS PILGRIMAGE

A poet came into the city
        which was the city of the world
               in a great smooth stream of traffic
     the sea urgent salmon surge of
           slippery, sleek, sharksnouted strangers.
               He was a country poet
  of no reputation (but a name to come)
           on pilgrimage to the CITY LIGHTS BOOKSTORE,
  borne on a fluid seaswirl of strangers
        lost in the city of the world,
               downtown, Chinatown,
        wall-to-wall sex of the tenderloin
           looking for a place to park.

The city received him oblivious,
      as the sea receives its ten million minnows,
          breakfast for barracuda
   and he walked among ten thousand chinamen
        women, babies, grandmas, wildeyed warriors,
           clucking their wierd tongues,
        on Grant Street bustling with meat-markets,
           everyone buying what they needed:
    ginger root, tripe, chicken, cabbages, fisheads.

And none of them needed poetry
      to mix with the soup or season the eggrolls,
         all went on haggling and bargaining
    laughing, eating, fighting, singing,
        taking ten thousand private shits,
           making unknown love to each other
        each with a private penis/vagina
           living its secret life
               in the city of the world
           with its wall-to-wall strangers
              sleeping on sidewalks
          panhandling, pandering
    in the daily, prosaic business of mankind.

The poet came into the bookstore,
      which is the bookstore of the world,
         through the black, narrow door
   into its augean bookstalls,
        narrow, winding,
           topheavy bookshelves
        bearing the soul of mankind
          as well as its bullshit,
        carrying the great names
          in slick, new editions
              floor to ceiling
          wall-to-wall poetry
             culled from the privacy
        of our great loneliness.

The poet sat down by the window,
        which was the window of the world,
              to read a few pages
      from one of the ten thousand volumes
            of the poem of mankind,
      awash with the great passion
              the grief and sorrow,
                    love, love abandoned and burned,
            the dark ships approaching,
                  raids on the inarticulate
                        who wander the streets,
                  sleeping on sidewalks
                        like lost sailors--
      what bodies, what passions, what lovers!--
            words, swimming like minnows
                    in silvery streams
            in the darkness of the soul.

The poet submerged himself and drowned
        in the darkness of the City Lights Bookstore
              which is the ocean of the mind,
      aflood with uncountable images,
            the songs and the dreams already in print,
                  hanging by their wings
      in the great meat-market
                  which is the market of mankind,
      and was happy to be drowned there,
              quietly sinking under the pressure
                        of the presence of great writers
              aware for the first time
                    how many swim under the surface,
                          how few find the light.

The poet walked out of the City Lights Bookstore,
        into the naked street
              with its wall-to-wall hunger,
      light pouring down between skyscrapers,
              between pylons of darkness,
                    carrying in his net a few books
            fished from the ten thousand titles
                  which he would never possess,
                        never read/never need
            in his small, secret swimming
      of the dark currents of nameless living
                  which are the currents of desire,
      and stepped into the stream of strangers
                  flooding by on the sidewalks
                        without looking at each other
            and disappeared instantly among them
                              without a word.

ON WRITING

It is late again. The fire burns down. My wife and the children have been asleep for hours. In the half-dark room, writing at the table, I hear the night noises of the house, the noises that surround my sleep--furnace, refrigerator, clock . . .

A car rushes past. Who else is up tonight? Only drinkers and lovers. A few insomni-acs curled around their mysteries. Grave shift operators. Perhaps another writer, somewhere in this city. Yes, surely there is another one, pushing pen across paper in some quiet room tonight. Perhaps with a small lamp by the window. A fire in the woodstove. A woman perhaps, finishing the last line of a poem.

My thought goes out to her--compatriot! Be strong tonight. Finish the damned thing. Good for you.

And the cat meows at the window, wanting to come in from the cold.

ADVICE TO THOSE WHO WISH TO BE FAMOUS WRITERS

Look--
if you hang around long enough
and don't quit writing,
people will eventually come to think of you
as a tradition--a monument--
even if your work is mostly garbage.

This really happens.
They will say: look how long this cat has been writing.
Look at all the piles of garbage this cat collected.
That's quite an impressive landfill.
Must be something in it.

So you become
established--famous, even--
for things done twenty years ago,
things that mean nothing to you now,
but which some energetic connoisseur of trash,
excavating layers of anthologies
will transform into an academic study
proclaiming you one of the great garbagemen of all time.

And you will be flattered,
and cantankerous,
and pleased as a pussycat.

GETTING DOWN

In the time that belongs to me
I go down to my writing room.

In the night,
after long hours at work,
after walking the dog
and being with my wife until bedtime,

I go down to my writing room,
this well of yellow light
underground, in secret,
lighting candles
as if it were the catacombs.

I go down underground,
under stress I
break down
in the night
in quiet candlelight
here, in my writing room

I get down,
I get down on my knees,
I get to the bottom of things.

POEM FOR THE POET'S WIFE

My body has been faithful
        but not my mind

My hands have been faithful
        but not my heart

My tongue, dumb servant of my
        heart and mind
        hangs out like a dog

My body belongs to you
        with its dandruff
        its rank odors
        its snoring all night

My feet will run marathons for you
        and my penis
        will do what it can

But my mind and my heart
        like childhood lovers
        make words to each other all night

ANNE SEXTON

You so much more than I resist
the greediness in others to devour
that soul in us that cannot be possessed.

I know another form of loneliness,
coming from the unchosen child in me
that cannot find cannot create a home.

You stare the demon down. I run and hide.
The poems kick to be born--they rage inside.
O proud, lost girl--we come from the same country.

AKMATOVAH

there is no legal audience
for your thoughts.

wrote poems
in those years
on cigarette papers
for friends to inhale
with the smoke
to keep truth alive.

the dictators are gone.

the poems survive.

BECAUSE I ALWAYS WANTED TO BE LOVED

That's all. It's that simple.

That's what lies behind the behavior--
      the endless flow of poems,
      the outrageous braggadoccio . . .

And because I am afraid of facing rejection--
      I always choose an empty auditorium,
      singing there to no one
      at the top of my voice.

WRITING ON MY KNEES

Writing on my knees,
Love poems are all I want tonight,
Pastoral songs of the ancient earth,
Hymns and psalms of humankind,
Beauty of innocent faces.

There are no innocent faces.
Weapons and hungers of humankind
Make a desolation of the earth.
Dirges are my only songs tonight,
Writing on my knees.

AT THE RACES

The poets of my generation are assembling.
They are lining up in magazines and anthologies.
It is becoming clear now who is in the lead.
Certain names show up constantly.
This one wins contests every year.
Another is forever receiving fellowships.
These have books out from major publishers,
their faces on the covers of poetry magazines,
crisp photographs, open, intelligent faces
of men and women giving their lives to poetry.
Some of them I know personally.
Others I know are not among them.
I am not among them
and that's okay.
Like thoroughbreds on Derby Day
they're pacing at the starting gates until--
BANG! THEY'RE OFF!--pounding toward immortality
and we cheer and watch with our binoculars
from the bleachers of the ordinary world.

REFUSAL TO MOURN THE PROLIFERATION OF POETS IN AMERICA

Why should they not spring forth like flowers
in every valley of xerox and mimeograph,
these little magazines filled with rare specimens?

Who told us to police the universe?

There is room for the cultured rose,
for tulips grown on thousand acre farms,
and room for dandelions on every lawn.

For mountain orchids also, springing unseen
in only one particular, hidden, private place.

Let them all come forth in abundance, as they will!
Forbid them not -- who can forbid them anyway? --
these transient blossoms sprung from excited brains.

Let us have poems sprouting from every crack
in the perfect asphalt parking lots of America!

READING IN POCATELLO TOWN

Pocatello is the reading place
if you're a poet seeking audience,
if you seek a crowd of eyes and ears
hungry for the dance of wit and words.

Rank and title you can leave at home.
Rather bring your dreams, your love, your fear,
flambouyant ego and outrageous rage,
death and murder dancing on the page,
unspoken pain and sacreligious tears--
they are all welcome here.

We are not charmed by name or fame,
or touring pros who play the game.
We have come to see the *real thing*
as we have seen it often here before--
the unknown southpaw from the minor leagues,
with a wicked sidearm curve as clean as Shakespeare.

So come as you are and become what you will,
for better or for worse, for good or ill,
speak your mind and stammer out your peace,
give whatever's in your soul release,
here, before an easy-going crowd
in poem-hungry Pocatello Town.

RIVERSTONES

for Will Peterson

The poems of your life are never lost.

They lie beneath the surface
                like rocks in a riverbed,
        polished by the rushing of your mind.

Now and again you stoop and pick one out,

turn it over in your hand,
                heft it for weight and size,
        run your fingertip across the grain,
                and toss it back again.

Then you stop and pick up this one.

It looks and feels right.
        Carry it home
                to be published in the rock garden.

ARS POETICA, DATELINE 2056

in a world of palmtop fingertip
supercomputing services
running on lightbeams

a man in a hidden room gets out
the fountain pen inherited
from his grandfather

and using a sheet of homemade
paper performs the
radical act

of opening his mind

WHERE POEMS COME FROM

1.

what can you do with your wild desire
but join the circus and learn to juggle fire,
soar on the flying trapeeze, strut the highwire,
dance with elephants, siberian tigers, polar bears,
ride white feathered stallions round the ring
in the bellowing bigtop, reeking of people and popcorn.

2.

the horses of ambition, once whipped
in galloping frenzy down twenty-five desperate years
stand free at the far end of a sunwashed meadow,
amid dandelion and thistles, nibbling windblown grass,
and the soul, on its back, half-asleep in the sun,
stares at clouds drifting across oblivion.

3.

there is a song one catches
walking a trail through an aspen grove
beside a mountain stream that is always singing
its solitary jugband melody mingled with birdsong
and the wind between two-hundred year old fir trees
blowing from snowfields cupped beneath granite peaks.

and none of this singing is for sale
or written down or saved for posterity
except in memory, linking light with sound,
weaving today and tomorrow with fallen leaves
where flowers that grow only in this place
break through the crust of a long winter
opening their golden centers to the sun.

that is where poems come from.

THE RESURRECTION OF THE WORD

They assembled all of us in the town square
    and brought out this old man.

He was charged with speaking poetry,
    a capital offence in our country.

Word whispered that he was the last poet.
    All others had been executed.

They made him stand on the wooden scaffold
    behind a bouquet of microphones.

"You must renounce your words," they said.
    "Renounce them before the people."

The old man looked out at us.
    Then he began to sing.

Before he sang the first line of the poem
    they cut out his tongue,

So he beat out the rhythm with his hands
    until they chopped them off with a hatchet.

So he looked at us with eyes filled with the poem
    until they gouged them out.

Covered with blood, tongueless, blind before us,
    he stomped his feet in a dance

and waved his bloody arms in the air
    until with gunbutts they beat him down

and still his booming heartbeat filled the square,
    so they cut it out with bayonets.

"The Word is Dead," they shouted, lifting
    his heart in the air.

Then someone raised the first line of the poem,
    another clapped and another danced

until we were all singing, clapping and dancing
    and the thunder of it brought the scaffold down.

Then the troops came in with the machine guns.

THE KINGDOM OF THE WORD

The disciples of the living word belong
to tiny congregations skilled in song,
not unlike the early church, that met
in catacombs, by candlelight, in secret.

We should not be discouraged to be few
in number, for this is always true--
that two or three will gather for a reading
drawn by common need, as to a prayer meeting.

The power of words to change our lives and heal
the wounds of loving--is alive--and real.

It cannot be coerced, controlled or bought,
or manufactured, mass-produced, or taught,
but is a gift, mysterious and free,
to all who suffer in the name of Poetry.

DYLANSONG

a poem for my grandson

Little fish, little beanpod,
whose eyes at six weeks open wide
    as the universe,
        blue as the Pacific Ocean,
           into a mind
              wide as the universe,
        clear as the sky
           above the Pacific,
    how do I sing you,
how do I tell you,
that love lifts a waveswell within me
    when I look in your eyes.

Tiny creature of time,
first-born of my first-born daughter,
    blood of my blood,
        whose eyes will see the next century,
          even in sleep
            you are listening,
        consciously feeding on sound,
as the ocean roars its dull roar out your window,
    how do I tell you,
        how can I sing to you,
          hope rising high in my throat
        like a lump of amazement
each time I hold you,
your long fingers curled in the fold of my shirt.

I am your grandfather.
All that I know about living means nothing here.
    All that I know about suffering
        washes away.
The debris of my windblown life,
        broken dream-fragments,
scatter the sands of my mind patterned with footprints,
    which the high tide of morning erases,
    unrolling a clean scroll:
        the perfect shell curve of your ear,
the crenelated edge of your iris opening on darkness.

All day I hold you,
        heartbeat to heartbeat,
small head tucked under my chin,
    asleep on my chest,
        as I travel through time

to a time I can hardly remember
when I was your size, asleep on the shoulder
of someone whose face is a mystery,
and others, whose faces are memories
hovered around me,
kissing, commenting,
touching my uncurled fingers
at the end of a war
in the bombed-out wreckage of Munich
where I was new as a daffodil
sprung up in a graveyard,
delicate, wonderful,
and the blessings they whispered,
the tears that fell on my forehead
as I slept on the shoulders of grandparents
stained and sustained me,
colored my soul
with permanent patterns of sorrow.

Oh! what to tell you!--
nothing! nothing!
rather tell me--
teach me anew what life is--
sing to me all the new songs,
suckling whistles and greedy wheezes
as you root for the nipple,
cooing, half-singing snores
as you sleep on your belly--
teach me anew what I knew
half a century ago,
and I will hold back
what I know
letting it come to you slowly
over the years, saving it
till you suck it from me,
thirsty for human sorrow,
songs out of loneliness,
war songs and love songs,
sagas of heroes and battles,
and mothers searching the battlefields
for their lost children.
These I will hold back till you need them,
(though they are real
and are your inheritance)
held in abeyance like a storm out at sea
while I hold you with both hands,
whispering blessings
and baptizing you with my tears.

* * *

This is the song I sing you
This is the mantra I lull you

(as you lie on my elbow
small arm around my back
breathing so gently
through such perfect nostrils
eyelashes flickering
on your curved, chinese eyes)

This is a grandfather's blessing
lulled in a deep-throated whisper

(while you lie curled
bean in a bean pod
close to my heart
feast for my eyes)

Let it enter your ears like a heartbeat
Let it beat in your blood like a mantra
Let it unwind its long silken string
like a prayerwheel turned by your dreams

I love you -- I love you
no matter what happens
no matter what comes

Come life, come death,
with every breath
I will always love you

As you grow--as you know
as you suffer the world,
as you wander and wonder,
wounded in confidence,
battered by lovesongs,
each day of your living remember

I love you--I love you
I will never forget you
your face is engraved on my heart.

* * *

You were born with the ocean in your blood,
the ocean that sings at your window,
Dylan, Dylan

Each morning while you are sleeping
(or nursing, or howling your head off)
I walk on the beach

reciting your name with the waves
as they roll thundering up the sand
to wash away footprints
with scallops of creamy foam.
Dylan, Dylan
is what they say back to me.

They cast forth their pieces of poetry,
crabshells and starfish,
fishing line, floats and shrimp skeletons,
long tubes of rubber-hose seaweed,
syllables, syllables,
pieces of life
pounded and punished relentlessly,
delivered into the hot sun
to feed seabirds.

The sandpipers of the spirit chase each wave,
racing the glistening edge of receding foam
to feed on fragments that the sea casts forth,
endlessly offering wave after wave these
voices, memories,
perfect sand dollars
unbroken and washed by the last wave,
spirit money from an unknown place
magically presented to scavengers
poets and grandfathers,
pockets filled with coinage,
fragments of transient beings,
smoothed pebbles,
silken driftwood,
Dylan, Dylan
your name.

And in the tidepools at cliffside,
by the hollow, wave-blown rock
where the breakers burst through
thunderous, boisterous,
the kelp fluttering backward
wavedrawn, waterdriven,
where starfish retract
and anemones grip stone,
there is always the surge of new life,
possibility bursting in,
sucking the old life away,
and I walked here
the week you were born,
gathering starfish, sand dollars,
stones of all colors
each with your name on them,
each singing new life,

Dylan, Dylan
          ebbing and flowing,
                    gifts from the sea.

Of death and dominion
          (sung by your namesake)
                    I shout to the breakers
that breakdown my syllables
          into shell fragments
                    booming, subsiding,
          shooting through rock caverns,
"Death and Dominion
          and Death shall have no--"
                    crashing and thundering,
                              rinsing the rocks.
And the gulls overhead cry
                    Liiight! Liiight!
          who are not poets
but scavengers, survivors,
they swallow anything,
          poverty, storm-wrack,
                    an abundance of garbage,
          death their dominion,
                    wheeling in sunlight,
                              on their white wings--
in your eyes gulls wheeling, waves sounding
                    Dylan, Dylan
                              soul of the sea.

                    * * *

I bring the greetings of generations,
          those I knew personally,
                    others in stories only,
          generations of grandmothers, grandfathers,
                    Oma and Opa
                              Ur-Oma, Ur-Opa
          back to the garden,
          their faces now in your face
greeting me as I stare at you sleeping,
                    welcome! welcome!
          all who are chained in your molecules
                    sing in your blood,
          fish people, bird people,
          clan of the turtle and grasshopper,
who knew life and had children,
          met death and entered the darkness,
                    entered the light of our memories,
                    sing to you, boy,
          your people, a host of them,

back to beginnings
                in Germany, Ohio, California
                    so many faces
                            appear in your face.

                We, who have suffered,
            who have known love and sorrow,
        who have lived through world war
            and poverty, hunger, the many despairs,
                    survived and passed through it

                        live now in you,
                know more than you can imagine
        of what lies ahead of you,
    holding back nothing, we bless you,
        go then, go into it, go
                in the stream of your yearning
                        found and forgotten,
                but never abandoned,
            even in sorrow, which all of us know,
    we are all with you, within you,
            helping you, strengthening you,
                holding you gently
        with prayers for all seasons,
                courage and wisdom,
                        love like a reservoir,
                            Dylan, Dylan
                    peace like a river,
                lean to us,
        trust us to help you,
feel us within you,
        family, ancestors,
                singing your name.

                        * * *

What else can I give you,
        out of this well-worn body,
                holding your body
        new as the universe,
ears hardly hearing,
        eyes scarcely focusing,
                we equal each other,
        touching with fingertips,
newborn and old man,
        ends of the moibus tape
                touching infinity.

If you needed my life
        I would give it immediately,
                heart, kidney, bone marrow,

liver, whatever--
        or maybe my stories,
                a gift from my mother
        given your mother
for you to give grandchildren
                decades from now.
Open your fist,
        take hold of my finger.
Open your eyes and take hold of my heart.

        O Dylan, Dylan,
                trust your old grandfather,
        trust life, all it offers,
                it's scars and its scares,
                        dark nights and bright days,
        sun, moon and stars
and all of humanity
        waiting to greet you,
                don't be afraid of it,
                        trust your old grandfather,
        walk out and greet it,
        take it with both hands,
love it and eat of it,
        drink its deep waves,
                ride through the seafoam
                        bathe in its saltwater,
                rinse in its tears,
        find someone, love someone,
trust your old grandfather,
        trust yourself also,
                give yourself utterly
                        to eyes and to faces,
        love will redeem you,
                more than all money,
        more than religion, technology,
more than all cleverness,
                love recreates you,
                        as love has created you,
        Dylan, Dylan
        strong as a seasong may
lovesongs surround you,
        forever and ever
                                we love you
                forever
        your mother, your father,
grandmother, grandfather,
        love you, we
                        love you,
                high tide or low tide,
        we love you,
        love you,

all days and always,

we love you,

love you,

love you,

love you,

love you,

love you.

BREAKDANCING AFTER FORTY

the mind breaks into pieces, things
break into shards, crumble in places,
words, the ideas they strutted forth,
shoelaces, lampshades, marriages
(though some stay together elastically
due to longsuffering forgiveness) still
my mind loses connections, breaking
synapses, shorting out, overloading
because i push myself wanting to die
fairly young, i suppose, broken in
every part by circumstances, except
in love, dear sweetheart, sustained
by kisses, old friends, children, dogs
and poetry, never a broken heart.

ADVICE FROM THE LOVE-WORN

When to married men in middle life,
the thought that they will probably never touch
another woman other than their wife
hits them sudden like a blast of air
that lifts the trembling branches of the heart
with gusts of anxious longing and despair,

let them recall the other side of sex--
the angry rage, the jealousy and doubt,
the suicidal urge when she rejects
all touch and talk, the silent hell
that lasts for hours--and know full well
those consequences they can live without.

Instead of chasing after some sweet bitch,
let them fix a cold beer and a sandwich.

ELEGY FOR AN OLD BLUE VOLKSWAGEN BUS

Old Blue, tonight you're in the boneyard
without your license plates, new snowfall
melting down your windshield. Fifteen years
you hauled family, firewood, assorted boyscouts,
teenagers, sheetrock, two-by-fours and friends
without accident and with much abuse, survived
both children driving you through high school,
had your guts torn out by amateur mechanics,
ate dust on mountain roads and navigated
one hundred thousand miles of interstate
and never hurt anyone.
                        I think of you,
with private sorrow saved for faithful friends,
old dogs, lost loves and certain battered
vehicles made beautiful by suffering.

THE MAN IN CHARGE OF MACHINE GUNS

has soft hands, like a concert pianist,
for he must play the obligatto
in the Death Sonatas.

The man in charge of handgrenades
wears weightless shoes, like a ballet dancer,
for he must skip and leap to throw
bright flowers to the audience.

The man in charge of atom bombs
sings in a high voice, like Pavarotti.
When he performs the swan song,
he sings for everyone.

We improvise our lives each day,
here in the streets and alleys,
softshoe, old guitar, close harmony.

TRUE STORY, MAY 23RD, 1991

Joyce Simpson was debating
whether to continue singing
in her church choir as she
was leaving a gas station
in Stone Mountain, Georgia,
and saw the face of Jesus
shrouded in spaghetti and
tomato sauce on a
billboard ad for Pizza Hut.

The face had deepset eyes,
a beard and a crown of thorns
staring out of a forkful
of steaming spaghetti.

She decided to stay in the choir.

IN THE SHOPPING MALL AT LYNDA MAR

A teenage girl "scores"
a pack of Marlboro's
at the liquor store,

runs out excited, laughing
to her friends in
the waiting car . . .

First cigarette, first
beer, first driving
fast, first sex

& the rest of it
as they say
is poetry.

HUGH HEFNER'S FACE

The oil of pleasure turns the skin
brown as a well-preserved cadaver's.

The lantern jaw with its clenched pipe
hangs between two buxom cottontails.
The sunken eyes above it stare
at the approaching, ultimate Playmate.

Neither gold chains nor fast cars
will prevent her touching you.
Already she reaches for your bowels,
your lung and heart, your private parts.

Lie down beside her pelvis full of dust,
her eyeless sockets, her virginal lust.
Accept a kiss from this eternal whore.
She is the one you have been waiting for.

MY FATHER'S FACE

his hands

never noticed before

nose quite large

and clear eyes

red around the edges

he pats the dog

his friend

then

looks up at me

TWO BY EDVARD MUNCH

SPRING EVENING IN KARL-JOHAN STRASSE

Parades of ghosts along Karl-Johan Strasse.
Hello! Hello! Cadavers! Ghouls! Werewolves!
Skeletal faces carved from blue-green cheeze.
Shrunken foreheads molded from old wax.

The living dead! Those smug, embalmed physiques!
How to bear to breathe the air they breathe?
Surrounded by these brownstone mausoleums --
Agggeeeeehh! I want to scream and spit at the sky!

Run through the crown - arms in the air - escape!
How did I come to be here? Where is my home?
Breathe shallow now. Be calm. Be one of them.
Swallow your spittle. Twist a manic smile.

PUBERTY

Night.

She has slept here
for one thousand and one nights

Awake.

On the edge of the bed,
naked.

Small breasts.

Hands that know what to do.
Bright eyes.

Shadows.

THE LEAVES FALL DOWN LIKE POEMS COVERING MY LIFE

I no longer think of failure or success.
The game is personal, excercised alone.
I think about the darkness between women's legs,
how sorrow hangs between the legs of men,
how mothers leave their boys to grow alone
and fathers chase their children through the streets
and sons wake up to wonder who they are,
years later, lost, in forgotten towns.
It is this darkness that I hunger for,
and sorrow like a secret, silver knife
and someone who will hold me when I die.

The poems fall down like leaves covering my life.

THE MAN WHO WANTED TO HELP

sat crying on the curbstone
with his head in his hands,
kicked by the beggars
as they stumbled toward soup kitchens
on the way to the grave.

He handed out food and they kicked him.
He handed out money and they kicked him.
He gave them new clothes and they kicked him.
He offered them jobs and they kicked him.

At last he just sat there
holding his head in his hands,
a man worth over a million dollars,
powerless to do anything.

And the beggars enjoyed kicking this rich man.

Thus, in his way, he helped them.

STRAIGHT, WHITE, MIDDLE-AGED MALE SEEKS A LIFE

It's like the whole world is wearing
        wild, colored underpants

                and here I stand
        in these plain old white cotton briefs . . .

I don't want to change,
        but it sure is pissing me off.

MY HANDS

two old veterans of the wars
with their fat companion

SURFIN' SATORI

all your words
                will wash away

        like the tracks of sea birds

                when the tide comes in . . .

HOLY WEEK IN SANTA CLARA COUNTY

The traffic goes by day and night.

Ten thousand restaurants are open.

The few remaining orange groves are blooming.

Semiconductors are blossoming like glass roses.

Jesus reflected in windows of shopping malls.

Even at midnight the traffic still roaring

the jets roaring overhead every hour

decibles penetrating concrete skin and bone.

Mardis Gras masks the Totentanz

in this carnival country,

hot grills frying meat, steaming shrimp,

hiding the black-boned back alleys,

the immigrant's face in the windshield,

parking lot crucifixions of the poor

and Lazarus resurrected in styrofoam.

Everything wrapped extremely tight.

BMW's, Porches roaring day and night.

BURNING BUSH HOLINESS CAMP

Every time I passed it driving to work
or home again at night on Wildcat Pike,
I felt an urge to stop at that old barn
(handpainted BURNING BUSH above the door
and wooden benches scattered around inside)
just to watch the righteous jump and shout.

It burned down one summer night--struck by
lightning or the wrath of God, who knows?
Only charred rafters and a black foundation
left as a testimony to firey preaching.
I hope it wasn't a cigarette snubbed out
in some corner, but something truly Biblical,
entering the folklore of the farms around.

Why didn't I stop when I had the chance?
I was too proud--uncertain, and afraid.
Afraid of tongues of fire praising God
and of the choices that my soul might make
if, by chance or miracle, on my knees,
I heard Him speaking in that still, small voice,
kindling the empty branches of my heart.

BEETHOVEN ON A BICYCLE

I was wandering,
andante sostenuto,
down a tree-lined lane
in the old cemetery,
when Ludwig pedaled by
on his black bicycle,
waves of hair sticking out
under his top hat.

Then mother was with me.
We walked beneath the trees
dripping from the rain.
It was the third time
she had visited me.
We didn't say anything.

There is a point
when the music turns
like Ludwig on his bicycle,
leaving the paved pathway
to wander amid the gravestones
spontaneous and delicate,
like the largo of the ninth symphony.

Orange and yellow leaves
were falling on all sides.
Ludwig pedaled through them,
one hand in the air,
conducting the silences,
while the other hand
rang a silver bell.

I was alone again.

ONE EVENING IN JULY

as I wandered around
the neighborhood
under a full moon,
people talking to each other
across their lawns
and kids riding bikes
in the warm darkness,
thinking how wonderful
this America, this
free place where
everyone is happy

in an apartment
across town, one
Mr. Sengthaviosouk,
laotian student,
shot to death his
estranged wife,
turning the gun
then on himself,
unsuccessfully.

how can there be
only one truth,
one reality?

CONCERNING TIME TRAVEL

I wake up in my father's house, in the south bedroom where my mother slept when she was dying.

It is a little after two in the morning. The full moon throws tree shadows on the bed. I get up and stand by the tall window. There is a stranger in the street below, looking up at me.

I know he is looking directly at me, don't ask how. It all seems natural and terrifying. The hair rises on my neck and arm. He has been watching the house for hours.

I want to call out, but cannot speak. I cannot move or make any sign to him. And then, for no apparent reason, he turns around and walks away under the streetlight.

And now I realize--it is myself--standing outside the house where I am sleeping. And part of me moves off into the darkness. And part of me lies down to sleep again.

BUZZARDS

generally two

or one alone

circling

on tipped wings

visible for miles

wherever you are

in Ohio, the

skyway patrol.

EARLY MORNING, SOMEWHERE IN OHIO

The white tongue-and-groove two-stories on Main Street
are dark now, huddled beneath their maples.

The empty square, lit by mercury vapor lamps,
is populated with parking meters.

Miles away, dull traffic of trucks and trains
rumbles like a distant thunderstorm.

Then, like a civil defense air-raid siren,
the soul of a citizen raises up into the night:

WEEEEAAAAAAAAAHHHHHHHHHOOOOOOOOOOO-O-O-O - O - O!!!!

A dog barks. A few porch lights turn on.
Then everything settles back to sleep again.

NIGGER HEAVEN

My best friend in the third grade lived there.
He invited me home to supper one night.

Broken house, tarpaper shingles, dirt yard
with a dog on a thick rope barking at everyone
and his dad asleep on a torn sofa on the porch,
a small t.v. turned up loud and blipping
and his mom who looked real tired
stirring noodles on the kitchen stove
and yelling at his older brother who
had locked a neighbor kid in the outhouse
and was threatening to burn it down.

I ran till my lungs burned up,
in tears, blind and hurting beyond words,
unable to share that meal or that life.

I was sixteen before the name meant anything.

ON THE FARM

Behind the run-down grain bins

where the fence opens into the alfalfa field

I almost stepped on a small, grey kitten,

ball of fur hunched in the short grass,

her eyes glued shut with disease.

She would have died there in the autumn night.

I carried her back to the house,

noticing how wide and dark the earth becomes

after sunset, the cool breeze filling my shirt,

and fields spreading back to the border of trees.

SAYING GOODBYE TO SKY

Evening in the backyard, early spring,

trees in new leaf (how often have I felt this?)

the sky clear as some rare, tinted glass,

and birdsongs from the fourteenth century.

I have crossed over a boundary in my life

the coolness of wet grass pulls me down,

and now it seems that we are saying goodbye.

THREE VIEWS OF NEBRASKA FROM INTERSTATE 80

NEAR LINCOLN

early evening fireball on the horizon

dreamy blue-green fields in purple haze

small, white, clapboard country church

short, black steeple and off to one side, the moon

like a bowl of creme on a velvet tablecloth.

COZAD

tall, white grain elevators ten miles away

like a greek temple in the clear morning sun

the name C O Z A D stands out in black letters

bohemians with scythes knee deep in the wheatfields

ABOVE SIDNEY

wind always blowing and combing the grass

bending the cottonwoods and the few scrub trees

the prairie dominates like a state of mind

human pretentions long since blown away

dig down deep with both hands hold on to survive

THE ENVY OF TREES

Because they are simply there
and that is enough for them.

Because they produce without instruction
leaves, create shade and are beautiful.

Because even in disintegration
they are lovely, generous.

Because though rooted here, they are free,
while I who kick through heaps of leaves

walking to work, am prisoner.

ANOTHER WORKING DAY

I envy the dog,
        who sleeps all day in the chair,

and the old white cat,
        who sleeps on a pillow downstairs,

and the goldfish in the acquarium
        on top of the piano . . .

As I put on my tie and leave for work,
        I envy them.

THE OPENING OF SPRING

To begin with, the nailed furring strips
that hold the plastic on the porch windows
are pried off in a celebrative shower of dust
and dried-up corpses of mid-winter flies.

Next the white caulk around the window seams
is split with a pocket knife and (at last!)
like pressing the stopper from a bottle of champagne,
the locked latch is twisted and the bottom tapped and--

      * * * * WHOOOSSSHHH! * * * *

Like a perfumed debutante, Spring enters the room.

We sweep out the corpse of winter with a broom.

WALKING AT NIGHT

It is October now.
The Dipper hangs in the west
and night comes clean and cold,
distilled from loneliness.

I walk beneath bare trees
in shreds of twilight blue,
crushing the brittle leaves
beneath my shoes.

Each house is huge and dark
with yellow lights.
No one looks out to see
who passes at night.

Above the rooftops rises
the harvest moon.
The dogs and I alone
possess the town.

FLOWERS FOR MARC CHAGALL

Painter of flowers and women, painter of love.

Today you enter the stream of souls you have painted
        all your life.

What can we say for you? What can we give?

Flowers! Flowers dropping their petals like tears,
        not of sorrow, but joy, of radience and light!

Your gift to us remains, mysterious, beautiful.

There is no dying for souls that have truly lived.

I take these flowers, not to some graveside or church,
        but spread them along the streets and give them away
        to women and men, singing your glorious visions!

I set a vase of flowers in my heart permanently for you.

Let me never be afraid or discouraged or defeated
        in spirit by those who work to destroy
        all the singers of joy -- NEVER!

You are alive and I am alive and the universe is alive.

The singing universe alive with flowering souls.

DARK DOOR FULL OF LIGHT

Falling in love is an affair of eyes.

We give ourselves to faces open as mirrors.

It has nothing to do with our bodies.

Dark eyes pull us hungry into the heart

where we know and are known more naked

(that is to say, more vulnerable) than flesh

by telling all we are without a word,

and giving all we have within a glance,

until, like diplomats from distant lands

come fingertips, and the first cool touch of hands.

THE DARKNESS WITHIN WOMAN

She turned her head slightly
and looked at me out of the corner of her eye
for only a moment, as ringlets of rich, black hair
bounced on her shoulder.

Her eyes were alive with interest,
piercing me, stabbing the heart of me,
so that my chest and my stomach were wounded, on fire,
and no one existed on earth except she and I.

She gave me her hand and led me into her darkness,
into a dark room far from the known world.
In darkness we took off our clothing
and her body glowed like an ember.

With my heart I fell into her darkness.
With my tongue I tasted her darkness.
With my fingers I opened her darkness.
With my manhood I entered her darkness.
Vast as the universe, wet and mysterious,
warm as the mother, and salty as oceans,
her darkness surrounded all parts of my body
and I gave up my breath to her kisses,
and I gave up my soul to caresses,
and I gave up all wish to return
to a life in the everyday world.

In the pale light of morning she left me,
exhausted and asleep on the edge of eternity,
as sunlight announced creation in sad detail,
the cracks in the plaster, the crumpled sheets,
the window panes streaked with the filth of the city.
I curled up and moaned for the darkness,
the wonderful, lost darkness of woman,
the gift of oblivion within her belly.

Then staggered naked and desolate into the street.

THE LOVERS OF SARAJEVO

in memory of Admira Ismic and Bosko Brkic, May, 1993

The last two lovers in shell-shattered Sarajevo--
a Muslim and a Christian Serb, Admira and Bosko.

Inseparable companions, created by God for each other,
hope of mankind, light of the world, these lovers.

Nor history, nor ten generations of hatred can harm
this man and the woman he shelters under his arm

from snipers and schrapnel in shell-shattered Sarajevo.
Their only desire--to find somewhere safe they can go.

Then one day they risk it--a suicide dash between armies,
almost succeeding--just thirty yards from safety

someone decides to exercise his machine gun.

Wounded Admira dies cradling her beloved Bosko,
the last two lovers in shell-shattered Sarajevo.

For six days they lie unburied out under the sun.

GIRL AT A BASEBALL GAME

Turn your face to me and break my heart.
And I thought I was too old for this!

Black hair curled around each ear,
tiny blue plastic earrings,
Nefertiti chin and classic lip,
eyes as wide and dark as mountain pools,
and breasts . . .
                              God help me.

There are girls like you in every town in Ohio,
legs spread on the bleachers in tight jeans.
One of the ballplayers perhaps will
put his hands there later tonight.

I go to push my children on the swings.

Ten to nothing, bottom of my life.

THE AURORA BOREALIS

My wife taps on the windows from outside.
"Come and see!" she says through glass.

Ten p.m., mid-September night. I leave
the desk scattered with papers, bills, letters,
the calculator, the computer and a cup of tea
to walk out into the backyard.

Between two trees that block the streetlight
we stand and look straight up, my arms around her,
the sky alive with colored, shifting lights.

"It's the first time I ever saw them," she says.
Twenty years married, alive and well in the universe.

LIVING IS WHAT WE DO WITHOUT UNDERSTANDING

Living is what we do without understanding.
The simple miracle of our bodies making love
to bring forth babies from between your legs
could never happen if we gave it thought.
Yet this tall man with hair hanging down his back
and two-days beard is twenty-one years today,
connecting us to each other and to the earth.
For you and I were born of lovemaking
and pushed out naked from our mother's legs
to grow and find each other and make love.
It is as mysterious to me as sunflowerseeds.
I stand in the garden surrounded by green leaves
in late evening light, aromas of soil and compost,
my toes sinking deep into earth without understanding.

I LOVE YOU VIVALDI IN THE TREETOPS

I love you Vivaldi in the treetops,
sunswollen cloudset midsummernight I love
over rooftops down alleys beneath dark trees
your dark arms raised above me and hair in my face
as I kiss you rolling on soft grass beneath stars
in a dream come true, your eyes, your legs and lips
open for me like white flowers in a painting of
lovers at night by Chagall we float like kites
over the violet city in a cloud of golden light
immortal as dream children, fragile and bright
in the mooncharmed moment of sensual abandon
beyond thought beyond fear beyond consequence,
tossed into space, blind, naked, wrenched, curled
about each other like the only two souls in the world.

WHEN YOU LOVE ME THERE IS ONE UNIVERSE

When you love me, there is One Universe.
All clocks tick in tune with our heartbeats.
I can believe in the Grand Unified Theory:
God, Eternity and the Harmonious Spheres.
Your love creates new worlds with every kiss.

But when we argue, and the silence comes,
you wrap the room around you like a field
that bends space, warps words
and sucks me into my anger
like a neutron star collapsed to a black hole.

The laws of love are relative, balanced by
quanta of forgiveness against uncertainty.
Jesus, woman--say those lifegiving words,
and let new light explode into my soul.

WE HAVE BEEN MARRIED FOR NINE THOUSAND DAYS

We have been married for nine thousand days.
What do we remember from that flow?
The day we met, the first time we kissed,
the night you said you loved me in the dark,
the first time we touched our nakedness,
the day and hour each child was conceived,
the night before we moved to Idaho,
lying beside you early Christmas morning,
an argument, a gorgeous day, the stars,
long mountain walks together and alone,
a few close dances at a cowboy bar,
our daughter's wedding, the time we prayed
for safe delivery through a blizzard for our son,
and everything else that happened, on and on.

WALKING THE FIELDS

for Jane

Evening now,
at the old family farm.
The eastern sky is chalked in blue pastel
as darkness begins its slow advance across fields.
A light wind stirs the grass and the washed-out moon
rises behind the abandoned barn and silo.

We walk far back in the fields,
you in a loose cotton dress with little else on,
me in my open shirt and old blue jeans.
The dogs run ahead, scouting the hedgerow for rabbits.
You pick some wildflowers--daisies and tiger lilly.
I pull out long spears of grass to chew on.
A langorous summer evening, soft and warm.

For a time we stroll apart, then our hands touch.
Far back at the end of the lane we stop and kiss.
I slip my hands inside your loose cotton dress,
the cornfields spin around us in a swirl
as we become the center of the world.

We grab a breath. The dogs come barking back.
The western sky swells rich with orange light,
and fireflies start winking in the mist
as we slowly walk back to the house,
the moon like a lost hubcap at the end of the lane.

HAPPY

my wife wants me to be happy
i want my wife to be happy
i cannot be happy if she is not
and she cannot be happy if i am not

my wife is happy
when she is at home
in the garden or sewing
or spending time with our grandson

i am happy when
writing poetry or walking around
with time on my hands or cooking spaghetti
and drinking wine with friends in the backyard at night

my wife teaches school
so that i can stay home and write
and cook meals and do what i want to do

i work in a factory
so my wife can stay home and sew
and garden and play with our grandson

as we work for each other's happiness
neither of us have much spare time
to do what we enjoy doing

we are both very happy

COLLATERAL DAMAGE -- FRAGMENTS FROM THE GULF

*"Turning and turning in the widening gyre,
the falcon cannot hear the falconer."*

> *-- W. B. Yeats*

*"We'll just put some bleachers out in the sun
and have it out on Highway 61."*

> *-- Bob Dylan*

ANOTHER TWENTIETH CENTURY DIRGE
ACCOMPANIED BY THE HEAVIEST OF METALS

|

the birds of war are flying into the desert
from all over the world, you can see them

the great, black helicoptors sit on the broken trees

(sit down in the ashes and weep, O parents
you parents and grandparents of young men,

the dark vultures lift off the heaving deck

the oiled, metallic thunderbirds hunch over us
with fire in their claws, they watch and wait

|

this line in the sand, January 15th

if we step back, the enemy grows strong
but if we don't step back, the carnage comes,
the carnage no one wants, or so we say,
yet none of us will step back, we or they.

since you're on your knees anyway,
        might as well pray.

|

(O where is that Mayor's *Prayer Breakfast*
        when you really need it?)

|

and the boys in my scout troop
are the right age to be eaten
by the thunderbirds
            my son among them.
for the first time
he asks me about vietnam
and why i didn't go.

what can i tell him?
                    i was lucky.
you be lucky too.

!

*now is the time to do something
now it is your turn, old man.*

*stand up against this madness,
speak out, march in the streets,*

*throw yourself beneath a truck
in front of the federal building,*

*wrap yourself in the flag
and set it on fire.*

or write a letter to the newspaper.

!

they bombed baghdad this afternoon
the news came over the radio at work

some collapsed while others stood in shock

i felt this way when kennedy was killed
not knowing where to go or what to do

!

*moonlight, pathetique, appassionata . . .
alfred brendel on the black steinway*

the damned, clipped precise comments
of cheney and colin powell describing
"surgical strikes" and "collateral damage"

next they'll get into body counts.
i know this cold, cutting wind
jesus, how i know it.

beethoven in a body bag.

!

and if it ends quickly
and if it ends in victory
o then we must mourn truly
          and not celebrate these deaths

they belong to us
our own dead, the enemy dead
they hang around our necks
          like a heavy necklace of severed heads

and if it does not end . . .
if the metallic oil-burning birds
consume our children in black pillars of smoke
          it will be the long-awaited end

          our nightmares come true at last

!

scud attack on israel.

in the afternoon a woman with fear on her face
comes suddenly to us--
                    "they just hit tel aviv"

earlier the noise of a passing truck
sounded like aircraft
                    and everybody jumped.

here in Idaho, it touches us

!

o christ, lord jesus, if you're going to come
please end our violence with your armageddon

save this poor, ruined planet from destruction
do not have mercy on us--we deserve none

blast all humankind to kingdom come
we are not worthy of your great salvation

pour oil on our faces, burn us down
until every vestige of our bones is gone

until the earth is free from domination
and all remaining creatures saved from oblivion

!

now our sons are dying

the first allied pow's on t.v.
ashen faces, ashen words
like ghosts that have crossed the river

a voice trills in my brain: *DO SOMETHING!*

!

i want to stand in the street and tear my clothes

i want to get down on my knees in traffic

i want to shout STOP IT! STOP IT! STOP IT!

instead i write a letter to the newspaper

!

also, i want to fly the flag
give blood for the troops
and kick the ass
of that smug son-of-a-bitch saddam

!

and in latvia, the soviets open fire

i put out my hand on the tv screen

mark a bloody cross on my forehead

mark of cain, mark of bloody war

!

today we are used to the bombing
soon we will be used to casualties

then the body counts begin
as governments keep score

as bite by gagging bite
we eat the war

!

questions not covered in the briefing:

when we bomb an iraqi nuclear reactor
where does the radiation go?
how can you tell an iraqi from an iranian?

from an egyptian? an armenian? an arab?
from a jew? *black moustache. fierce eyes.*

will there be internment camps in idaho?

how many barrels of oil does it take
to fill the persian gulf?

how many bodies does it take
to fill the gulf between us?

how many deaths will it take till we know, etc...

!

i feel the thunder of bombs
dropped on cities like mine on people like me

i see the dead stretched out in the street

suddenly out of the clear sky
a scud missile screams toward my house

i spread my arms apart to receive it

!

our president is calm in his resolve
our generals and commanders are calm

they are confident in their plan
they have achieved the upper hand

yet the bombing, the relentless bombing
continues and continues and continues

do not ask. do not wonder. do not sigh.
just tie a yellow ribbon around your eyes.

!

when do we get to see
the suspected v.c.
his head blown off
by a snubnose pistol
on national t.v.?

!

pentagon says "prepare for a long war"
the toymakers are happy

business is BOOMING again

TIME-LIFE is taking subscriptions
for the GULF WAR eleven book series

!

and in a small, worn corner
the fabric of america unravells
beginning on a sleeve, like new england,
then the midwest and southeast pull apart,
the mississippi dries up, unzipping the country
like a body bag and california falls out

we hold hands while we sleep, holding our breath,
holding the country together with desperate threads
we accidentally bombed an air-raid shelter in baghdad
and all night long they carry out the dead
the patchwork falls to pieces in our sleep

tomorrow the ground war begins

!

not a yellow ribbon but a green one
worn across the chest, across the heart

for all the life being damaged and destroyed
as we consume the planet and ourselves

!

each evening we watch the game

poker, not chess, they are playing

tank battle in Basra tonight

from our seats in the electric colloseum

we cheer for the home team to win

!

isaiah 30, verse 29 to the end

schwartzkopf, blackhead, wunderkind

jonathan winters in uniform--i love him!

100,000 iraqi soldiers buried by bulldozers

but it's over . . . over . . . over

!

the war has ended
you can stop eating now

just a little "mopping up" to do

the midday smokeclouds of kuwait
the fires of hell in the human heart
slivers of schrapnel slicing everyone

is islam the true faith?
is allah the true god?
is jesus christ victorious?
will el shaddai deliver us?

the beaches littered with dead birds
nineveh and babylon, cradle of civilization,
firebombed in the mother of all battles

change your channel back to "normal life"

the war has ended
you can start sleeping now.

!!!!!!!!!!!!!!!!!!!!!!!!!!!

TONIGHT THE WAR BEGINS

It is snowing heavily.
I sit in my basement room
listening to Polish folk songs
and writing in the blue notebook.
I am fighting off despair
like Polish partisans
fighting off the Naziis
in the snows of 1944
and there is nothing for us
but to have another war,
to start terminating people
with our "awesome firepower"
out in the Arabian desert
where grunts snuggle up to their guns
and the bitter sandstorm blows
its rhetorical blizzard.
Christ it is lovely,
this snowfall laying down
at least four inches tonight
and I want to walk into it
as into another world--
Kenton, Ohio, in 1950,
"year of the big snow,"
when war was a comic book
and father made snow ice-cream
in the safe, warm house on Detroit Street.
Mother, a war bride, survived
the small town prejudice,
only me to remind her
of bombed-out Munich,
snow covering brickpiles,
people foraging firewood and food
and everyday rebuilding
so that Die Frauenkirche stands
brand new again and the
newborn never know
the stain of war.
My son's generation
with their blurred inheritance,
surreal mythologies of Vietnam,
stare into the television,
knowing this is no movie,
their future gobbled up
by destiny. And tanks
are crushing partisans
in Vilnius tonight as
we stand by watching
Lithuanians lay flowers
on those poor, dead faces,
and somewhere in the desert
wave after wave of fighterbombers fly
to drop smart bombs on houses made of clay

on those who waited too late
or were too poor to buy
their way out--
                    Jesus!
                    I want you to come tonight!
Like the Bible says--now--
before any more people die--
come in the Rapture, the Perousia,
gathering living and dead into the sky
like snowflakes flying backwards
and thus fulfill the scriptures
so our suffering can be ended
and all the non-human species
(what's left of them) can
live in peace at last
on this soiled planet
before we destroy it completely--
                    but no--
the Prince of Peace
is sitting this one out
while the slaughter begins
in the name of peacemaking--
                    I put on my coat
and walk into the wordless swirl of snow
beneath canopied, snow-covered trees,
past the houses of my friends,
musicians and artists, the
emergency room doctor
and the man who has already
shoveled his sidewalk three times,
the young couple with their newborn son,
thinking tonight about this war coming on
like tanks rolling down our street,
ponderous, black, shaking the pavement,
and I slouch angry, desperate
into the heart of the storm,
the snow falling and the night falling
soft and beautiful as death on our sleeping faces.

DON'T LIE TO ME

I am tired of being lied to.

By government leaders, leaders of industry, their paid
        spokespersons, spokespersons of civil authority

By newscasters who emphasize that part of the round truth
        that is paid for and sells newspapers

By people afraid to tell the truth because they will lose
        their jobs, their homes, their lives

By religious hucksters who set up God like a coke machine

By bureaucrats at all levels who lie for the fun of it
        because they have secrets no one else can know

By doctors and lawyers who keep me in the dark to protect
        my feelings and postpone the inevitable

By friends who are too polite or kind or wrapped up in
        their own problems to risk confrontation

By teachers who have already surrendered their values
        and so each day surrender a bit of the truth

I am tired, I say, of being lied to--and of lying to
        myself and to others.   It is wearing me out.

But the Truth which is priceless is free for the
        speaking, but ah--it costs much--it costs
        everything.

I will pay it. I have nothing to lose and can accept
        nothing less than the Truth. Here is my
        body, my blood.

        Don't lie to me.

POEM FOR MARIA ELENA MOYANO, FEBRUARY 1992

. . . assassins shot her in the head
and lit a dynamite charge to destroy her body
as friends and relatives looked on in horror . . .

A black butterfly flew out of her purse:

"Death is pursuing me," she said.

Leader of the Glass of Milk Program

in defiance of the Shining Path,

On Friday she addressed a rally in Lima:

"We are not with those

who kill popular leaders,

who massacre leaders of soup kitchens."

On Saturday they shot and mutilated her.

How little of the terror happening every day

in poverty and isolation

is made visible to us.

One voice raised up like a banner.

one brave, bright soul destroyed.

Remember Maria Moyano,

who gave one million children

a glass of milk.

SAINT JUDAS DEJAVU

New Year's Day.
I walk to the post office
to mail some bills and get away
for a few minutes from the relentless
review of the year's bad news,
faces of starving Somali's,
corpses in the streets of Sarajevo,
rain washing corpses out of the muddy fields,
unending misery, cruelty and violent death,
at the end of this most violent century
of great technological advances
(like nothing seen before)
all faithfully reported on 38 channels--
look at it!--just look at the world--
oil-soaked, ozone depleted, battle-scarred--
between afternoon football games . . .
So I walked out, sick of it all,
to the post office, as I said,
the cold air cutting through my coat,
when I came upon an old fellow
sitting on the icy sidewalk
right in front of the post office
with his feet in a puddle of slush,
no hat on his head, no gloves,
coat open to the bitter wind
that was blowing white hair into his eyes
and I almost turned away from him,
not wanting to face yet another
human tragedy--

                        when I realized--
this one is real. This one
is here. This one
belongs to me.

"TELL THE PEOPLE IN THE PARK"

The young woman shot dead after she broke into the University of California chancellor's house carried a note demanding a halt to construction at People's Park. The woman, best known by the alias Rosebud Abigail Devono, was shot three times Tuesday after she charged a police officer with a machete . . . "We are willing to die for this piece of land. Are you?" read a note found inside a dufflebag.

Joan Baez in concert on PBS tonight.
  Short, smart hair, good nose job, bit of a
    doublechin, but still looking *good*,
 the clear voice cutting through the bullshit,
   she sings to my generation,
     the balding, paunchy, graying crowd
   clapping hands and swaying together,
(we were in high school when Kennedy was killed)
   singing 'bout FREEDOM, FREEDOM,
    and I sing along,
     folding clothes & watching the tube
   with moist eyes,
    that old idealism still alive.

Meanwhile, Rosebud Abigail Devono,
   age nineteen,
  is shot to death in Berkeley,
    charging the security guard
  with a machete in her hand.
 She made a phone call from the hallway:
"I'm at Tien's place. They're
  going to shoot me.
   Tell the people in the park."

Old Joanie singing and the flower children
 swinging and swaying together,
   "FREEDOM, FREEDOM . . ."
  and later,
    for Rosebud,
 a song that is always true:
   "It's all over now, Baby Blue."

THEY ARE CUTTING DOWN THE TREES

They are cutting down the trees
that lined the road behind the cemetery,
willows and elms, most of them,
trash trees, good for no purpose,
yet beautiful and sheltering to those
who walk or run here at all hours of the day,
cheered by sun on the icy branches
or new leaves in the early spring,
or the golden blaze of October afternoons.
All this has been methodically cut down
and I run through a wickerwork of trimmings,
the raw, freshly fallen trunks still wet
and stumps pushing out moisture as if alive,
chainsaw fumes still fresh in the morning air.

Of course I have no right to be outraged.
Those who own them, city or university,
can do whatever they please with land and trees,
but the wet stumps speak to me with open wounds
as I run against the rhythms of the chainsaw
cutting through ancient rainforests in Brazil,
bulldozers pulling out scrub juniper with chains,
and butchering these worthless willows and elms.

I am convinced that those with power over trees
are threatened by such covered, hidden places
where people can escape and live alone.
They want them cleared away so to control
each hour of human life, leaving no privacy.
For that alone, we must stand up to them.

And for the trees who cannot say their pain,
who have no tongues, but suffer all the same,
peaceful beings, ripped into, chopped and torn
with living water running out of their veins--
who will stand up and be their advocate,
defending their right to life and dignity
against the powers that process property?

I will do it. Will you stand with me?
To join the movement, simply plant a tree.
There are many of us in this country.

THE WEIGHT OF THE WORLD

you see it in the eyes
       looking from side to side
       anticipating trouble

and the hands flexing fists
       unconsciously, ready
       for action

a sudden noise and we flinch
       looking over our
       shoulders

the newspaper and the tv
       weigh us down
       with news

we know too much about disaster
       and the unspeakable
       things people do

the world is a heavy overcoat
       we put on every
       morning

and wear to bed each night
       beneath thick
       comforters

the stress of violence
       in our daily
       lives

no matter how secure
       we seem to
       be is

       killing us.

THE PRESENCE OF THE MURDERED ONES

Each night the murdered ones come to the house.

Look out the windows and you can see them.

Those who have been murdered by their governments,

herded into mass graves and machinegunned,

burned to death in public, starved in prison,

pulled from their homes at night and "disappeared."

They stare at us while we are asleep

until out of nightmares we wake in a cold sweat.

Because of this it is impossible to rest.

There is no peace in our cities or towns.

We see our precious ones torn from our arms,

attacked by vicious dogs and carried away.

We stand in tears by the window as the world burns up

like a paper rose tossed onto a bonfire,

and together with the murdered ones we wail

in high, thin voices out of our tortured sleep,

crying *Mammaaaa! Mammaaa!* although it is too late.

OUR HUNGER IS AN ENORMOUS HOLE WE ARE TRYING TO FILL

We sit for hours feeding at the television.

Fill me with dreams of all I dare not do.

Give me an uzzi and let me blow people away.

In my ferrari I speed down the hairpin turns.

Hotbreathed and lovely, she opens her body for me.

Give me the ultimate mindfood, virtual reality.

Yet even in cyberspace I am never fulfilled.

All of this fighting and fucking leaves me empty.

Where is the manna that will restore my soul?

Where are the loaves and fishes to feed five thousand?

Where is the bread of life I cannot control?

It comes as a gift to those who will let go.

I never let go, instead I go for the gusto.

I gobble up all I can dream of, all I can see.

That is the future my hunger prepares for me.

FOR THE JEWISH HOSTAGES MURDERED IN MUNICH, 1972

Let us give up all talk of dying and death,
as well as explanations of the universe.
Terror has shattered our world like the breath
of God in a whirlwind we cannot reverse.

Later will be time to touch names carved in stone
and the inarticulate trunks of the holy trees,
to wander deserted dirt roads, bewildered, alone,
and breakdown in tears in the long grass on our knees.

Into our festival houses the killers have come,
wearing black masks to compete in a deadly event,
the world their stage and television their weapon,
they waste no time in slaughtering the innocent.

Hear O Israel, the Lord our God, the Lord is one!
Vengeance is mine, says the Lord, and mine alone.

MAYDAY, 1975

The bread of innocence sours in our guts.

Like the man who finally committed adultery,
we bought a one-way ticket for that train.
Before it left the station, we believed
we could get off at any whistlestop.
Once in forward motion we became
the helpless victims of our vanity.

No artifical slogans can deceive
the grim reflection in the midnight glass.
The nightmare we denied has come to pass.
Our own momentum drives us through the dark.
And what was once a nonchalant affaire
becomes a bed of thorns to pierce our heart.

We lean against the window in despair.

THE WALL

not as big as I imagined
yet it fills the earth

(the weight of 57,000 names)

along the gravel path
loveletters, locks of hair

christ--even a snapshot of a '57 chevvy

in early morning hours
when no one watches

those whose memories are so fierce
they can't be trusted to daylight

sit on the hill and weep

they push their prayers into the cracks
and talk out loud to unforgotten friends

(kissing the carved names)

kissing their own faces
reflected in darkness

IN TIANANMEN SQUARE

the Idea, unbreakable

    though in its palpable

        paper-mache expression

    clearly vulnerable

        to tanks and machine guns

stands in the bloody square

    still visible

        for those with eyes

    as young, excited voices

        echo across stones

            for those with ears

you can crush, burn, obliterate

    these symbols

        eyes, ears, voices

            know what they share

Liberty lifts her torch

    in Tiananmen Square

CANDLES AND BULLDOZERS FOR THE BERLIN WALL

The bulldozers are coming to the Berlin Wall.
Forty years they have been ponderously approaching
through the black forests of an undefeated heart.

But first the candles come, cupped between hands,
carried from both sides to meet at this barricade
and climb it together and stand like a wall of light
in joyous reunion, closing the wound of the war.

Here are white candles for those who dreamed this day.
Candles of bloody wax for the thousands who died.
Thousands of candleflames transform the wall to a shrine
where people in tears offer prayers for a thousand names.

Then come the hammers and pickaxes chipping the edges.
Then come the sledgehammers, jackhammers joyously dancing.
Then come the ponderous bulldozers breaking it down.

TO THE KEEPERS OF LISTS

You keepers of the lists of enemies,
you accountants of those who must be killed,

I am your enemy. Put my name down.

When you come in the night with the black cars,
when you come at high noon with your machineguns

come here first. Take me first.

Without people like me your world is worthless.
And we resist all that you stand for with every breath.

ANTI-NUCLEAR CANDLES IN THE RAIN

At the Peace Movement potluck dinner
we shared casseroles and bread and beans,
sang folk songs, hymns and read Psalms
and danced a liturgical dance depicting holocaust.

Then we lighted candles in dixie cups
and processed silently out into the rain.
We marched up a hill to a small grove of trees
where we sang "We Shall Overcome" together.

We walked back to the chapel in heavier rain,
(hatred, bombings, murders in many countries)
and from a souped-up pick-up speeding by
someone yelled out at us: FUCKING COMMUNISTS!

How soon will they come with their black boots
and stomp out all the candles in the world?

THREE POEMS ON PAINTINGS BY TIM NORTON

THE FISH THAT WAS PREGNANT WITH NIGHT

The stars dropped through the mirror of the lake
to sift like luminescent shrimp in midnight water
until the cruising rainbow gathered them.

The moon floated crisp as a caddis fly
on the boundary between three worlds.
The trout erupted like a breaching whale
and was reeled up into the sky.

Reality is a dream fish cruising forever
the milky darkness of the universe,
swallowing galaxies, spawning moon and stars.

THE FISH THAT GAVE ITS COLORS TO THE OUTSIDE WORLD

In the beginning was the trout,
and the trout swam in darkness
containing all rainbows,
unable to see itself
until--with one creative SPLASH!--
it shook its colors into the emptiness
(broken like mirror-flecks on water)
and disappeared in a rush of blue,
cascading through yellow leaves, across
red stones, down white pummel of rushing sluice
and into black sand and long, green, underwater weeds,
declaring all of it good.

THE FISH THAT JUMPED TOO CLOSE TO THE SUN

At high noon on the summer solstice,
the trout had a religious experience.
It saw the bright sun penetrate the water
and knew it was a child of the light.

Responding with primordial homing instinct,
the trout thrashed up the waterfall of sky,
beating its tail against the foaming clouds
until it crested into the burning disk.

Like many a pilgrim swallowed by a god,
the trout remains a prisoner of the sun.
Its desperate leaps appear as solar flares,
and sunspots mark where it falls back again.

ON THE PORTNEUF

Late September, down by Whiskey Mike's.
From where I sit by a sharp bend in the river,
my line curving fifty yards downstream,
I can see Haystack veined with its first snow
and sunlight pouring bright as molten steel
out of the cloudless blue.
                      Shirtsleeve weather,
no mosquitoes or flies. Just the heavy drift
of clear green water running the riffle of rocks
and bits of watercress tumbling under the surface
where long strands of algae like wavering beards
wait to snag my hook somewhere downstream.

The water fills my thinking, pulling me apart
into the gentle and disconnected noises, willowleaves
blowing against each other, burbles and splashes,
the sun broken into jagged bits on the water,
so that I relax completely, even the desire
for enormous trout smoothed out and washed away . . .

A golden eagle circles overhead.

                      On wide wings
he enters my imagination, dominant, representing
all that Idaho has come to mean:
                      freedom, clear waters,
wild places, fragrance of aspen and sage, silver
rainbows laid in a creel of grass . . .

                      Thirteen years.

I have been here all my life.

WALKING AROUND POCATELLO AFTER DARK

These narrow, strange, beautiful streets,
idiosyncratic flowerbeds behind sagging fences
blooming with cosmos, zinnia, iris and marigold,
these impudent gardens of rambling pumpkin vine,
cucumber, zucchini, swiss chard and tall, festive onions,
lascivious leaves licking the picket fences,
these broken sidewalks with grass filling the cracks,
frontyards with birdbaths, ceramic deer, flamingos,
these lived-in houses with worn-out furniture,
where real people celebrate their lives.

SUN VALLEY

It's so refreshing, after the seemingly
endless parade of beautiful, gaunt aristocrats
in chic, expensive jogging suits and suntans,
to see, in Giacobbi Square, one genuine housewife,
a bit plump, wearing yellow bermudas, with her hair
tied up in a bandanna, pushing a grocery cart
between the BMW's and Porches in the parking lot,
to load two sacks of ordinary bread, milk and vegetables
into the trunk of a battered-up, blue 1967 Pontiac.

TEMPORALE

They drove up this afternoon
and for hours the canyon has echoed
with punctuations of hard rock from big speakers.

Now it is two a.m.
The Milky Way expands across the sky
and the wind plays its own long-practiced music.

Tomorrow the only trace of them
will be a dozen crushed beer cans
and a whisp of smoke from their abandoned fire.

SKIING UP CLEAR CREEK

On all sides: pristine, unmarked snow.
Air so cold this morning it hurts to breathe.

Up in the blue shadows, we stroke our way,
silent save for the rhythmic puffing and gliding.

We follow the sunken path of snowmachines,
our tracks the first to break the powdered crust.

At Boundary Trail, the canyon opens into sunlight
so clean and beautiful there is nothing to say.

The entire valley is absolutely still.

CAMPING ALONE

Sunlight
and a bicker of birds.

Pull on cold shoes.
There is frozen dew on the long grass
and air crisp with sage-scented mist.

Make a small fire.
Smell the rush of water in the stream.
Then bacon and eggs, coffee, a pan of biscuits.

Quietness collects on every side.
Your concentration
is complete.

Senses tingle,
like any natural creature
whose thoughts flash faster than words.

WE WALK ON ANCIENT LAND

The dry clay and cedars,
canyons of sandstone where a few aspens cling
        in the shadow of the windward slope.

Cliffs remote and silent,
mountains eroding away for millions of years
and the sky always changing overhead.

Underfoot--broken shells from the seabottom,
bits of bone, antler, skeleta and scree,
flakes of obsidian, knerled stones.

Dust of the ancient ones who lived here.

        listen!

        listen.

They are all around us.

GRAVESHIFT IN THE HUMPING YARD

Midnight--
moonlight ices the reefers.

Early June, but cold enough
the pin-puller on the hump keeps his hands
tucked under his arms, waiting for
a deuce or trey.

Down in the bowl the cars drift quiet as death,
moving toward you like an iron fist
to slam KAWHUMPH! into the the waiting train.

When the boys in the towers muff one,
you have to drag that cut-of-cars back through the
retarders, making the metal-to-metal squeal
like whales singing in the night.

By five a.m. the skyline's black on blue.
Light sifts into the east above the warehouses.
The boys ride back in the cab of the yard engine,
swinging their lanterns as they drop off at the shack.

Stop in at the Whitman for a beer and a bite to eat.
Pocatello, Idaho--working for Uncle Pete.

MOVING ON

The yellow frame house that stood for fifty years
between five cottonwoods at the edge of potato fields
outside Chubbuck, is ready to move to Pocatello.

Supported on two I-beams on wheels, it passes
one last summer night under the moon.   Tomorrow
it will roll on down the road, just like the
man who built it, moved back to Wyoming,
and the family who sold it to the realtors
because they found a job in Arizona.

After the foundation collapses, the topsoil
will blow away and wash into the Snake,
ending up eventually in the Pacific.
Even the young mountain range to the south
will be somewhere else in a million years or so.

What, then, is poignant about an old yellow house,
as lonesome as the last cowboy in Idaho
smoking his last cigarette beneath
the enormous, peach-colored, temporary moon?

SWIMMING IN SILENCE/DROWNING IN LIGHT

Sunlight enters

           the white skull of the sheep
through sockets open to air

                 my skull
should be that empty

             shot full of
pure sunlight

&

the stream rushes

      RUSHES!

how long has it been pummelling?

carving these black canyon walls
washing soft silt down the mountain

&

waterwashed pebble
round as an opal
what can you tell me?

darkveined traveller
from the earth's center
what will you give me?

thoughts are dust
wisdom crumbles like dust

&

i am young
        (i am nothing)

nothing gathers in me
but light crashing through like water
thunders it away

&

anger the need to kick
things to shout and shake

i want to be among trees
to lie in long grass
beside unspeaking rocks

&

water has been rushing all the time i was
writing these words

                    for days before i came here
and for years before i was born

                            (i who am so
young on the earth)

               nothing can hold
that much water

                    (RUSHING! RUSHING!)

mountains of melted snow

&

when i am among people
the deep longing to wander far away
comes over me like a music made of water

&

at the top of the footpath up the mountain
light falls simply onto the broken shale

&

i have been alive twelve thousand mornings
my heart has pulsed over one billion times

(to what purpose? to bring me here)

&

the longer i am silent
the closer i become

THE DISCOVERY OF SILENCE

First, you have to hike in, set-up camp, fish the stream,
climb all the rocks and sniff around like a hunting dog.

Then, on the third day, you settle down.
Sit in the sunshine for two hours after breakfast.

*

Clouds drift over the canyon wall like buffalo.
There is continual noise from windblown branches.
The nearby stream churns its splashy music.
Flies and mosquitoes zoom in and out.
Underneath that, you feel the Silence.

*

Things come together in your head.
You have not spoken aloud since yesterday.

The frantic pace of city life seems strange.

Now you are relaxed and at home,
companion to water and trees.

*

Silence like clear water enters your body.
Silence washes the round stones in your mind.
The peace of quiet trees stands tall inside you.
You stretch your hands to touch this solid stone:
The Silence of a world without mankind.

AT MY GRANDMOTHER'S GRAVE IN HAGEN

What you have given me
        cannot be measured.

Knowing that you loved me
        no matter what

has carried me through trouble
        and beyond despair

as the ocean swell lifts
        a small boat over the rocks.

You were my distant audience,
        and confidant.

When mother died you brought me
        to my birthplace.

We grieved and gossipped together
        by candlelight,

and walked each evening in the
        English Gardens.

We are one flesh, one spirit,
        you and I,

dear Oma, whom I remember
        until I die.

A WEDDING CANON

for Jennifer and John Nollner
August 5, 1989

The wedding at Cana, the couple so clearly in love
sit under the canopy centered in music and dancing,
their families and friends all feasting and toasting with wine
this union of two lives knotted together: a blessing.
And off in the courtyard, back in the corner, the Master.

The couple, though honored, have little thought for the Master.
They ride with their eyes on each other the crest of their love.
The guests file forward with gifts, each giving a blessing.
The bride and her bridegroom graciously govern the dancing,
till one of the servants whispers: "We have run out of wine!"

"No wine? It's impossible! Surely we have more wine!"
But the empty amphora are more than the bridegroom can master.
Embarrassed and helpless he stops all the feasting and dancing.
"Can anyone help to preserve this first day of our love?
To be without wine at a wedding is never a blessing."

Then, through the panic, Mary responds like a blessing.
"Go to my son in the courtyard if you need wine.
Do whatever he tells you in the name of God's Love."
Doubtful, but desperate, the couple approaches the Master.
When they look in his eyes, they see the whole universe dancing.

"Fill the amphora with water and go back to your dancing.
One taste of this new vintage will bring you a blessing."
The guests are amazed and go off praising the Master:
"Never in all our experience have we tasted such wine!"
The couple kneel to thank him for saving their love.

"O Lord, may your Love be forever dancing
within us, between us, filling us like new wine,
a rich blessing, a miracle from the Master."

DANCE OF THE DOUBLE WEDDING RINGS

for Jonathon and Carolyn Wyndham
August 7, 1993

The wedding of a woman and a man,
because it is not good to live alone,
begins, as in a dance, by taking hands,

and, looking in each other's eyes, you stand
before the presence of the Great Unknown,
who lives within each woman and each man,

and promise to be faithful to the end,
through all the steps and missteps that may come
by holding firmly to each other's hands,

this promise made before the gathered clan
of generations in the blood and bone
who circle round their woman and their man

with prayers and blessings as the golden bands
are placed upon each other's fingerbones
and two become one flesh, one heart and hand.

This is a mystery we scarce understand--
the folding of two separate lives in one
begins, as in a dance, by taking hands,
the marriage of a woman and a man.

AT PACIFICA

i hold my grandson
in my arms,

upstairs, in the nursery
i give him a bottle,

rocking to the roar
of ocean waves.

now more than ever
i think of you

mother and father
long passed away

who are enormous
horizon clouds

the ocean itself
surrounding

supporting as i
who am already

memory in his mind
touch both ways

connecting him to
the generations

blessing, blessing
waves on the sand

your faces above me
gentle, invisible

we sing him to sleep.

THREE CANDLES IN A DARK CATHEDRAL

For mother, who died years ago
on earth, but is not dead to me.
We touch fingers to the glass and
search each other's eyes in the dark room.
Be with me always I invite you, please.
There is emptiness inside me you can share
and loneliness for me where you now are.

*

For father, the staunch, lonely old fighter,
who built the house he lives in by himself
and walks from room to room gathering
the ghosts he wants to join for all time.
I think of him standing at a window
in early morning, waiting for the
signal to cry. I give it to him.
Weep openly. Be peaceful now.
You are forgiven.

*

For myself also, a candle. I would be
no longer all the things I dreamed to be,
but rather glow with God's light in my eyes,
the flame of Holy Spirit on my tongue,
and love for all that live within my heart.

THE ANNUNCIATION

I was standing in line
beside a black stone wall
in the pouring rain.
I had been standing
there for hours
with many others,
waiting to enter
the iron door
when the woman
in front of me
who was short as
my grandmother with
a worn, plaid scarf
over her hair, turned
slowly, as often occurs
in dreams, to face me
and it was mother.
I spoke slowly,
as if underwater.
"Your first grandson
is born. His name
is Dylan." She
looked into my
eyes a long time
and smiled without
saying anything, then
turned into the iron door
which closed behind her
leaving me alone
at the wall in
the rain.

MOTHER AND I DO THE DISHES

It's eight p.m. on a Sunday night.
I'm in the kitchen finishing the supper dishes,
the Cleveland Symphony playing something from Brahms,
the white cat by the door, licking herself,
Jane downstairs, grading papers.

Mother comes to me.
It happens often this way.
Perhaps the music invites her
or memories of the bright kitchen years ago,
the domestic peace of washing and drying plates,
that we shared whenever I came home from university.

I feel her beside me at the sink,
and break down, eyes blurred, throat
too thick to speak what can't be spoken,
as it is when I think of my own children,
wrapping their lives in my prayers.

Bubbles wink in the dishwater.
She is looking sideways at me,
but I cannot turn to see her face,
the dark eyes, the smile that I love.
Instead, I bite my lip to keep from sobbing.

It has been twenty years.
A space, wide as Montana, opens inside me.
Memories rush strong as a wild, thawing wind.
Mamma -- I miss you. We're still married.
The kids have turned out fine. I wish
they could have known you.

We hold hands across the universe.

Then, slowly, she withdraws.
The room shrinks back to itself.
I wipe my eyes with the dish towel.
The announcer introduces the 6th Symphony,
and the white cat stretches, wanting to go out.

AT HER FUNERAL

I held up well, I remember,
deliberately standing back
inside myself, not coming close
while the right hand shook hands
and the distant lips said words
(what words I can't recall)
to every face that entered
the funeral home with its
deathly breath of roses
and her body not there,
but cremated, so no one
could look at her face
in the casket. Then
Inge Dominick walked in,
who had been her friend
and confidant in the first
hard years after the war,
two brides from Europe
in a small Ohio town,
and before I could catch
it my soul leapt out of my
throat and my eyes caught fire
and we stood there holding each other.

WAKING AT NIGHT IN MY ROOM

Once in a while, awakening at night,
especially summer nights with the window open,
my hands on the blanket edged with silver moonlight,
and, far away, a freight train's monotone . . .

I stare around in the familiar dark,
disoriented and loosened, mixed in time.
The old black dresser thrusts its comforting hulk
against the blue flowered wallpaper of my room.

Bewildered, I don't know how old I am.
I hold my breath. A closet doorknob gleams.
Trucks roar past the house. Am I six or sixteen?
Have all these frantic years been just a dream?

For one clear moment, I know myself, and weep.
Then sink, like a tired swimmer, into my sleep.

ALL SAINT'S DAY

You have become
a weatherbeaten stone
whose name I cannot read
nor clearly remember your face
so crisply carved in pain.

Yet you are more real
than any photograph.
I kiss the rough grain
of your cheeks and lips
and speak your name.

All that remains is love.

ORDINARY LIFE

Aside from the perpetually unreeling illusion
of three hundred channels of actors in surreal stories
accepted eventually as parables describing our lives,
five billion people on earth go about with their ordinary
living and dying off camera without fanfare or fame
or even their names in the local newspapers except
to be born and married, divorced, arrested and buried
in funerals that only a few people care to attend,
and I take great comfort in this--how the billions
of unique faces and names are forgotten except for
a carved stone, aluminum marker, stick in the ground,
face in the family album to note we were here,
and that's wonderful to me--how common, superfluous,
everyday, nameless like sparrows and grassblades and
the everchanging clouds in the sky we are--you and I.

AMBITION

If I can't win Olympic gold
or write the greatest story ever told
or sail an open boat around the world,
conduct the philharmonic, star in a film,
earn the Nobel Prize for literature,
save millions of lives with a miracle cure--

I can at least stay married to my wife,
and raise our children to maturity,
obey the law, support the common good,
earn modest wage, pay taxes and plant trees,
be a good citizen of my community,
live simply, injuring no one.

That is not insignificant, though small.
It is the highest calling of them all.

MARRIED TWENTY-FIVE YEARS

for Carl and Joanne

We're all so respectable now
with our late model cars paid off
and a good roof overhead, clipped lawns,
every appliance known to man in our kitchens.

I remember drinking Boones Farm wine
and playing euchre until midnight
near the woodstove in your tiny kitchen,
windows steamy and our kids all horsing around
while we bitched about the government and the war,
our jobs, inflation and how hard life is.

How lucky we have been, the kids now grown,
married or working to pay off that first car,
that we survived it all and stayed together.

I sit in the kitchen, wondering how you are.

PUTTING AWAY THE OLD YEAR

So full of days and hours, it has become
a dry bouquet to press in the family album.
Condensed to a dozen photographs, the year
seems scarce old enough to have begun
and now it marks its final twenty-four hours
with music, letters and walks in the cold air.

We are medieval, deep in our middle ages.
The kids are grown and life is opening up
new opportunities, if only the world survives
and we have health to dance another decade.

We open the new year up like a ream of days,
waiting for the newsprint of our lives.
Who knows how many sheets we'll write upon?
Who cares? Love, let's begin with this one.

MY SON GROWS WISE

He learns to catch with one hand
        the heavy door closing behind him,

learns to weigh adult eyes
        for their grain of leverage

learns the tricks of tears and constant questions,

learns to fill his pockets when no one is looking,
        and fill his pants in a quiet corner
        and other pleasures--

        the benefits of sibling rivalry,
        lording it over children younger than he,
        climbing out of the crib one hour before
            anyone is awake
            to terrorize cupboards,
            raid the refrigerator,
            use forbidden hammers,
            eat cigarettes . . .

He is strong and healthy
        with a good-natured, crafty eye.

Even the old ladies whose doorbells
        he pushes constantly
        whose china bowls he bounces
        down the stairs, love him.

He is all cuts and bruises, bright eyes, smiles.

I am confident that he will survive
        the world's chicanery,
        the old shellgame
        and come booming out
        with good luck in his hands.

What worries me is--can WE survive
        his boisterous romp,
        his joy and sorrow?

Hold onto your hat, sweetheart--
        he'll be three tomorrow.

GLORY : GLORIA

for Jenni and the Pocatello Indianettes

When you give yourself totally to the dance
you enter for a moment Eternity.

Concentrate. Concentrate.

Only the music. Only the pulse of the music.
Remember to count. Move to the music and count.

Concentrate. Concentrate.

Not just alone, but together with fifty in
harmony, separately moving in unison: one body

Concentrate hard now.

Dance -- O to dance is complete freedom when
dancing together in harmony, unison, perfect!

(remember to CONCENTRATE)

FLY NOW! LEAP TO THE SKY NOW! BE BORN!
Never a moment like this one--a time without time!

con. cen. trate.

O prizes and trophies mean less than nothing compared
to the glory, the glorious moment, dancing in perfect

GLORIA!

Beautiful
                    (keep concentrating)

                                        Joyous

Complete and you've done it.

                                        Smile.

NIGHT BEFORE MOVING THE CHILDREN TO CALIFORNIA

The moon is full tonight, luminous
as a lemon drop, the sky softened by it
as we load the U-Haul truck with furniture.

When we moved out here in seventy-one,
the furniture and the kids belonged to us.
Now we belong to them. We pack twenty years
into the truck, along with tables and chairs.

Twenty years from now in California
(or wherever they are by then--who knows?)
some moonlit night, touching whatever is left
of all this worn-out wood and upholstery,
they will stop midstep, remembering us.

At least, tonight, that is my fantasy.

THE FULL MOON OVER THE APPLE TREES

throws a gentle light on the garden,
making the onions glimmer in their rows,
and on my face turned up to face it square.

The dog and I enjoy cool aftershowers,
the air magnified with honeysuckle, wet soil
and sweetness of the neighbor's linden tree in flower.

I wonder at this rich, deep peace I feel,
my parents dead, my family all but forgotten,
my wife asleep inside and the children gone.

To be alive with darkness and moonlight,
pulled from the house to stand in a timeless place,
surrounded by trees and vegetables, things of the earth.

It gives me assurance in spite of all wordly strife.
This is my house and garden, my moon, my trees, my life.

SONNET FOR MY CHILDREN

For you my boy, and you my girl, I give
from a loving heart full measure while I live,
that you might learn to laugh as well as cry
and dance with arms thrown up against the sky
in daily celebration of joy and health,
regardless of career, success or wealth,
for Beauty, which costs nothing and abounds
on every hand, on every inch of ground,
cannot be purchased with a rich man's purse
or squeezed into philosophy or verse
but must be danced to music--lived as art--
the province of a bright and hungry heart
for whom the world's a dazzling mystery
and love hangs ripe in every human eye.

POEM FOR MY 35TH BIRTHDAY

The sun celebrates my birthday at high noon.
Light! Light perpetual! Illuminated Son
of the Most High, bless me now I pray.
Penetrate, possess me on this day!

I give my life to you, Lord of pure light,
as it has always been yours each day and night,
except before, unknowing, I boasted mine
that which now I openly confess is thine.

I have no life without thy grace, great God,
no breath, no sight, no hope, no livelihood,
am less than dust, absurd and meaningless,
except thou lift me up with lovingkindness.

O once so dark, so fierce and proud--my heart
belongs to you, split open in every part.

PRAYER FOR THE HOUSE

Be with the dwellers of this house,
O Thou being of light and dark,
Thou maker and unmaker,
bless these lovers,
open doorways, guard their paths,
lead them safely out and home again,
keep them happy in each other's eyes.

As children come to them and grow
bless their perfect lives also
with the confidence of being loved,
so whatever else may come,
in the ambitious traffic of the world,
they do not lose each other
but are gathered daily into the heart,
into this house, into the circle of love.

CHRISTMAS 1981

I took a Christmas walk in a bitter storm.
Bundled and scarved, I braved the smashing wind,
trudging through heavy drifts as soft as sin,
and shouting out carols to keep my spirits warm.

The wind cut to the bone and I was tired
of struggling against the subtle weight of snow,
battling a gale that shattered my bravest song,
and so I rested beneath an evergreen.

Protected from the worst the wind could do,
I discovered the silence that my soul desired.
The tree stood solid as the hand of God,
creating stillness in the midst of storm.
The Holy Spirit spoke its Living Word,
as in my heart, the Christchild was born.

CHRISTMAS 1982

Out of our world of weapons, war and disease,
We yearn for you, Lord Jesus, Prince of Peace.

Out of exhaustion, weary of conflict and strife,
We hunger for you, Jesus, Bread of Life.

Out of our fear of sacrifice, out of our greed,
We remember you, Lord Jesus, Lamb of God.

Out of the sickness that wastes us without and within,
We pray to you, Lord Jesus, Healer of Men.

Out of our ignorance, out of deep moral distress,
We turn to you, Jesus, Teacher of Righteousness.

Out of despair with our lives--empty, absurd,
We ache for you, Lord Jesus, Living Word.

In expectation with people all over the earth,
We gather around you, Jesus, at your birth.

CHRISTMAS 1983

Oh dark, dark, dark, dark and dark
is this poor broken world tonight.
The threat of holocaust holds us by the throat,
and terror roams our streets with random bombs.
The prisoners of power enslave the poor,
and money and illusion rule the rest.

(Now--from the Living God--a Living Word!
Love! Love! Love! Love! and Love!)

Jesus Christ is born! He is alive!
He lives in all who turn to Him in need.
Beyond all doctrines and beyond dispute,
beyond the prison bars of mind and heart,
His all-forgiving love, made flesh tonight
is Light, pure Light, unquenchable, living Light!

CHRISTMAS 1984

O cover the earth, Lord. Cover it like snow.
Come in the darkness when we are asleep.
Transform the world with whiteness soft and deep.
Transform us also, as we dream and grow.

When we awake, Lord, let us be new persons!
No longer angry or bitter, overwhelmed with pride.
Overwhelm us with your Love instead,
that we might live each day in your Kingdom.

Tonight especially, this Christmas night--
O vast, mysterious Father, Creator and Lord,
be present here among us--speak Thy Word--
gather us speechless before Thy Perfect Light.

The Light of Jesus, in whom we are reborn,
be both our daily bread and daily passion.

CHRISTMAS 1985

Each evening I walk out in the snow
to tour the neighborhood transformed with lights,
the houses twinkling with an inner glow
of cheerful celebration--wreath on the door,
festive tree in the living room window--
and I am pleased (against the dark of night)
to notice that the homes of rich and poor
are equally made beautiful and bright.

So it is when Jesus enters the heart,
to stand within us like a glowing tree.
His perfect light casts out all fear of dark
and spreads into the night for all to see,
that strangers pushing toward some distant place
might find the Christchild in a human face.

CHRISTMAS 1986

When God entered into His creation,
risking the vulnerability of the flesh,
He did not come as King of all the nations,
the Prince of Power, conceived among the rich,
but rather as the poorest of the poor,
to common folk who struggle for a living,
He came to know the hardship, share the chores,
and experience for himself the pain of loving.

To Mary then--a simple, honest girl--
to Bethlehem and to Nazareth was born
the King of Kings, rejected by the world,
the Lord of Lords, who wears a crown of thorns,
the Prince of Peace, the Shepherd of the lost,
who carries all creation on a cross.

CHRISTMAS 1987

To see His birth in the birth of every creature
is to be religious. Not to see Him at all
is to be profane. We live and die
by how we see the world--bless and kill
by what we choose to know--God's Truth
made flesh for us in human faces.

Though princes of the world preach might is right,
and smooth-tongued preachers sell a cheap salvation,
the hard wind scatters them all like leaves.
Nature, unornamented as a tree, receives
our tiny gods like Christmas decorations.
The Lord arrives like fresh snow in the night.

Each living being contains all mysteries.
Approach each other, therefore, on your knees.

CHRISTMAS 1988

All children come from God. The power
to create human life is His, not ours.

Ours is to receive the precious gift
(flesh of our flesh, naked and helpless)
to care for with all joy and tenderness,
with discipline that is love's handicraft,
modeling mercy and demonstrating truth
despite our shortcomings.
                              To be completely *there*--
feeding, teaching, sheltering from harm,
suffering the unfair arrogance of youth
with godgiven patience that all parents share,
(the old man wrapping the prodigal in his arms)
this is the highest calling in the world--

to see in every child the Christchild.

CHRISTMAS 1989

We cradle round the tree of memories.

Long years after childhood is gone,
our parents gone, the children grown and gone,
the long walk after dark through snowbound streets,
beneath bright stars that reaffirm our dreams--
the box of handmade, fragile ornaments,
the colored lights and wooden crucifix,
two painted angels and a manger scene--
this glowing center of the midnight room,
a candled, caroled, memory-laden tree,
is rooted in a longing old as time:
to be alive forever in the mind,
to be with those we love and safe from harm.

To be the Christchild, rocked in Mary's arms.

CHRISTMAS 1990

In the barren winter, snowswept and bleak,
the heart opens its storehouse of good gifts
and entertains the Christchild in each guest,
spreading the snow with sunflowers for the birds,
with nuts and apples for the hungry squirrels.

We think about the hungry of the world,
about the millions that we cannot feed,
and how there is no war in wintertime,
when frost reminds us of our fragile lives
and how, but for earth's greeness, we would die.

In winter solitude we dream of peace,
a place to sleep in front of a warm fire,
where we forgive the injuries of the year
and are thankful just to be alive.

CHRISTMAS 1991

Walking with the dog one winter night,
worn out by overwork and by the world,
I heard a raucous unexpected cry
and saw a flock of snow geese in the sky.

Their ranks were ragged, not an arrowhead,
but more a half-bent bow of beating wings,
struggling west against the coming storm
and calling to each other for encouragement.

I felt their weariness and caught their hope--
the snowswept grainfields finally in sight.
I thought of winged, angelic messengers
proclaiming wondrous joy one starry night.

I thought about the long-awaited child.

Then turned to face the bitter wind--and smiled.

CHRISTMAS 1992

The Child among us -- this long awaited Child!
Child with eyes of innocence open wide
who looks into our faces without fear,
without prejudice or hatred, accepting each one,
whatever our age, our history, our color, whatever we are
this Child looks into our faces and sees what we are,
swims deep in the pool of our hearts and touches us,
this Child of God dreamed of for so many years,
come in the night in this unexpected place,
this place of poverty transformed into joy
by the eyes of this Child accepting all that we are,
our pitiful mistakes invisible, our sins unseen,
the world transformed and reborn and surrounded with peace
in the eyes of this long dreamed of Child of God with us at last!

CHRISTMAS 1993 *

A.
God was not born in a church or cathedral,
God was not born in a temple or a mosque.
Rather God came as a blessing to all people,
born in a manger in a stable in the rocks.

God did not come to the king and the rulers,
God did not come to the wealthy and the strong.
Rather God came to the wise men and shepherds,
and to the people who'd been waiting for so long.

B.
God did not come to the white people only,
rather to all men and women, yellow, red and brown.
God came to comfort the poor and the lonely,
and to free the prisoner, unjustly put down.

C.
God became a baby, helpless and wonderful,
Yeshua Immanuel, born in Bethlehem.

*To be sung in the style of a Hebrew folksong.

IN HEAVEN

In Heaven we will all be pleasantly surprised.

In Heaven everyone will be received --
        prodigals, exiles, saints, sinners -- all.

In Heaven we will not be afraid.
In Heaven we will welcome each other --
        gladly, forgetting all bitterness.
In Heaven, we will get to tell our stories
        and everyone will listen,
        crying at our sorrows,
        smiling at our theories,
        at what we thought was real.
In Heaven, everyone will be holding hands.

In Heaven there are no outsiders, no untouchables.
In Heaven everyone stands clean and beautiful --
        each in our own color,
        all the colors of light spread out
        in a spectrum of faces and voices.

In Heaven we will not recognize our enemies --
        Jew will not recognize Arab,
        Irish will not recognize English,
        Muslim will not recognize Hindu,
        Catholic will not recognize Protestant,
        Serb will not recognize Croat,
        American Indian will not recognize White Eyes,
        Black African will not recognize White African.
        It will not matter there.
In Heaven we will see each other for the first time
        and we will embrace and love each other.

In Heaven we will meet our mothers and fathers
        and all generations before us.
In Heaven the lost children will come home.
In Heaven there will be no religion,
        no need for philosophy or science.
In Heaven the answers will be obvious.
In Heaven there is no hunger,
        no unfulfilled, aching emptiness.
In Heaven even the rebellious heart will feel at home.
In Heaven our heavy coat of suffering falls off,
        along with our crowning achievements.
In Heaven we are completely known and accepted.
In Heaven each performance is applauded.
In Heaven there are no flags,
        no national anthems,
        no crusader hymns.
In Heaven all music is one syllable.

In Heaven there is no memory of Hell.
        Hell is where we came from.
        Hell was our proving ground.
        In Hell we learned forgiveness.
        In Hell we were broken and restored.
        In Hell we suffered and punished each other.
        In Hell we fought and died for our differences.
        In Hell we were never satisfied.
        In Hell we possessed one another.
        In Hell we abused one another.
        In Hell no one ever gave an inch.
        In Hell no one was innocent.
        In Hell we did what we thought was right.
        In Hell we never listened to anyone.
In Heaven, we have left Hell behind us.

In Heaven we never say God's Name
        or any of the ten thousand sacred Names.
In Heaven we are surrounded by Being,
        sustained, permeated, made incandescent
        by the Presence within and without us.
In Heaven there is no beginning, no ending.
In Heaven the Great Wheel stops spinning.
In Heaven we are finally ourselves
        without need to be important
        because we are in God.

In Heaven all of this makes perfect sense.
In Heaven all of this is a great mystery.
In Heaven we sit joyfully together,
        mixing and blending,
        touching and sharing,
        becoming one body,
        becoming one mind,
        silently together,
        patiently together,
        forever and ever,

        In Heaven.

ASH WEDNESDAY

Gentleness.

           Gentleness is first.

Then touch and blessing with hands,
and forgiveness
           sensed rather than spoken,
the eyes give it: safety, a secure
dwelling place where anger will not
explode,
      a tender glance that knows
all fear, suffers all wounds, sees
how broken we are,
           and for nothing
puts an arm around us and
leads us gently into
this warm circle.

           The Lord--
betrayed, deserted, beaten, crucified,
hurt beyond imagining--Himself
the creator of all--

           RISEN! ALIVE!

invites us to pick up our brother's cross.

MAKING PEACE WITH EVERYONE

Out of deep weariness with conflict, comes the desire for peace.

Not because we are too weak to struggle, or because we
	are cowards, but because we are tired of being
	always on the attack, tired of living behind
	walls, behind sharp words.

There is more to life than destroying the opposition.

There is something gentle, that lives without competition.

This is what we seek to find in others.

And so we come to make peace with everyone.

Peace with father and mother, forgiving their dominance,
	and with brothers and sisters, rivals for affection.

Peace with our enemies, forgetting our differences,
	wanting to sit down together and listen to
	each other's stories.

Peace with those who are hungry and poor, who envy
	our wealth and wish to destroy us because we
	do not share, or so we fear.

Peace with those who are selfish and pigheaded
	because they do not care about who they hurt.

Peace of the Savior, crucified, hanging before us,
	reminding us of our cruelty to others.

Peace of the quiet Tao, the Way of the Universe,
	conquering ten thousand things
	without making a move.

So we risk peacemaking, stretching forth our hands.

We deliberately smile and seek a smile in return.

We take our time and wait patiently on the others,
	for peace does not come naturally to us
	but it is well worth the wait.

Thus we live in a new way, alive and vulnerable,
	coveting nothing and sharing everything,
	calm from an inner core of personal peace.

Thus we accomplish peacemaking on the earth.

THE CHOOSING

Immaculate peace surrounds me.

Music! Violins! deliberate

and gentle, lifting, insisting on

resolution of disharmonies

until I am quiet within myself,

completely calm and confident.

No one can hurt me now that I know

the purpose I was born for has become

the living that I fit completely in.

I will affirm, uphold, create.

There is no other way to happiness.

LYING OUT IN THE LAWN CHAIR UNDER THE TREE

Above my face long strands of delicate leaves,

the weeping birch in mid-summer late afternoon.

I have been sleeping perhaps for an hour.

Waking is like floating up out of a deep pool,

the tree above me, caressed by a light breeze,

behind it cream-blue sky with smoky whisps.

Nothing moving, within me or without me.

The presence of the living tree pendulous above me.

We have belonged to each other long before time.

There is no death, no dying, no end to it all.

I ASKED FOR WISDOM AND ALL I GOT WAS THIS T-SHIRT

to suddenly KNOW

what i am is

particles

bound for a brief time

the soul singing

against emptiness

of atoms in space

and the universe expanding

at the speed of light

And then these enormous

silences

THE SOWER OF SEED

Actions before words--
live what you believe.
Then share with syllables
scattered like small seeds.

Each heart hears differently,
some not at all.
The Word grows quietly
where it falls.

Move on--you will not
pass this way again.
Leave tomorrow's harvest
to the whirlwind.

TO SEE THE FACE OF GOD

would destroy us

>   all possibility
>   present at once
>   on all levels
>   swirling beyond
>   imagination

brings madness

structures breakdown

>   our little world
>   systems so clever
>   turn meaningless
>   spin off into the
>   babbling darkness

He is merciful only

mooning us

SURROUNDED BY ALL I TAKE FOR GRANTED

Saturday morning seven-thirty, waking up late,
birdsong and a clear sky filling with sunlight,
cool air in the curtains and the dogs barking,
and my wife nuzzled deep in her dreams beside me,
I think of the world that has rushed around all night
with its traffic noises, crashing trains and sirens,
its blazing stars and its full moon touching our blankets
while we slept oblivious and safe in this comfortable bed
and the billions of cells within us refreshed themselves
carrying on processes to purify bloodstream and bowels,
sorting out yesterday, filing it in the deep closet
of seventeen thousand days and dreaming nights,
and so little is needed of me to make this happen
(the apple trees take care of themselves in the dark)
that I get out of bed like a cherished son of god,
pull on some clothes, use the toilet, feed the cat,
step out the backdoor barefoot into the sun,
dazzled by dewdrops that bless the tomato vine,
and all the undeserved miracles moistening my life.
I lift up my hands, close my eyes, receiving them,
while on everyside the universe vibrates its lovesong.

SEVEN BEATITUDES AND A PRAYER

1.

Blessed are you when the long hours of the day are opened like a book for you to read.

Blessed are you when the thick atmosphere reveals unfolding layers of scent and light.

Blessed to do nothing but breathe and feel, to hear, to see, to be silent and to understand that which cannot be put into words--the language of water, the voices of trees.

Blessed to spend at least one day of your life **alive** to a child's universe.

Blessed among men and women are you

> to stop one day
> to sit one hour
>
> to be in the presence of God.

2.

Blessed are you to be unaware of your body, for that means enjoying good health.

Blessed are you when you celebrate life in the body, rejoicing at the miracles of sense, appetite, emotion.

Blessed to move freely, to see, to touch,
> to know cool air, summer heat,
> to feel at home in the flesh,
> to enjoy simple food and drink,
> your body an instrument of sensual pleasure.

Blessed to learn humilty through illness and pain as the flesh forsakes you.

Blessed to learn control as you master the hungers and yearnings of the dust that separates you from God.

3.

Blessed are you when your heart is a reservoir of light.
Blessed are you when you have nothing to hide and step out of the inner darkness.

Blessed to have opened yourself before God.

Blessed to live simply, to confess failure,
        to own up to desire,
        to intentionally wrong no one,
        to seek forgiveness for all injury,
        to stop keeping score and forget all bitterness,
        to live simply, depending on God for all things.

Blessed are you when any weather is good weather.

Blessed to sing out loud and walk with a vigorous stride,
joyfully, swinging your arms.

Blessed to open yourself to the flooding light that surrounds you at all times.

4.

Blessed are you when your intellect expands and explores.

Blessed to conceive and arrange, analyze and remember.

Blessed for intricate patterns of changing relationship bound together in one
memory, one love.

Blessed to be unafraid to speak out,
        to push to the limit
        to recognize the limit
        to turn and return.

Blessed among men and women to know the kindling moment of creative thought,
to celebrate the intensity of making the new thing.

Blessed also to know that the mind is dust that blows away through the empty holes
in the eyes.

Blessed to open the intellect to the wind that blows through the branches of dreams,
holding on, letting go, caught in the drift of a big wind.

5.

Blessed are you to be surrounded with people to love:
    mother, father, sister, brother
    children and life partner, lover
    husband and wife.

Blessed to support and nurture, to care and to touch.

Blessed also to be supported and cared for and touched.

Blessed to **know** that someone knows you and needs you.

Blessed are you to be satisfied with relationships,
    needing nothing from outside,
    and, if needing independence and freedom,
    knowing also when to return
    and being accepted back with joy.

Blessed the arguments, the struggles, victory and defeat,
    the mealtimes, bedtimes, storytimes, quiet times
    in a home where people love each other even
    when they do not always agree.

Blessed when you know how rich you are and desire nothing other than what you have been given.

6.

Blessed are you when your work gives you happiness.

Blessed the achievement of the individual,
    who points at something and says:
    that's my work,
    that's because of me.

Blessed are you when your work is boring and unhappy if you overcome despair by singing in your heart.

Blessed when you work hard and rest long for your rest is like cool water washing a smooth stone.

Blessed when you toil at a task you hate for love of others without anger.

Blessed when you come home from work refreshed to begin your life work.

Blessed are you when your work fills only part of your life and you leave it behind to begin living at home.

Blessed when your life work and your living work are one.

7.

Blessed are you if you know how to love and be loved.

Blessed are you when you learn to forgive all injury.

Blessed because you travel light and bring fresh life to everyone you meet.

Blessed if you feel the great thirst of other people to be known, listened to, admired, cared for, loved.

Blessed if you desire nothing more than the giving to others of time, of listening, attention, touching, love.

Blessed if you know that nothing is more real than
      one to one listening
      one to one touching
      one to one sharing

Blessed above all if you allow yourself to be loved by those who need someone to accept them.

Blessed to accept and receive the humble gifts of those who are heavily burdened with love that no one wants.

Blessed to know nothing is more real than relationships.

A PRAYER FOR ILLUMINATION AND PEACE

Lord, let me open myself to your light.
Let these prayers be wide flung windows and doors.
Let my work be light labor, joyfully accomplished.
Let me learn to sing at all moments, everyday.
Let me be humble enough to listen and be loved.
Let me be silent in thought before the light.
Let me put nothing in front of you--
>> not desire or appetite
>> not career or ambition
>> not obsession or habit
>> not family or friend
>> not worries or fear

Protect me from the nibbling distractions.
Clear away all that separates me from you.
Remove all self-imposed darkness and despair.
Split me open clean and ripe as a melon in the sun.
Let me be filled with light, O Lord of Life!

>> Amen and amen.

OTHER BOOKS OF POETRY BY HARALD WYNDHAM

Rain Wakening, 1970

Epithalamion, 1971

Love & Marriage: A Sonnet Cycle, 1973

Down Home Ballads by Chalmers Furgeson, 1974

From the Asylum, 1975

Pebble Creek, 1978; Confluence Press

The Exile's Pilgrimage at Christmastide, 1979

Exile in a Cold Country, 1980

Cheap Mysteries, 1981

Strong in the Spirit, by Chalmers Furgeson, 1983

Homeland, 1984; Blue Scarab Press

Ohio Gothic, 1985; Blue Scarab Press

The Mount Moriah Studies, 1989; Blue Scarab Press

Kathedral, 1990; Blue Scarab Press

Prodigal Psalms, 1991; Blue Scarab Press

When You Love Me There Is One Universe, 1991